Contents

KW-326-766

Introduction

Preface

4

The Policy, Organisation and Rules of The Scout Association

Frank Stewart

Part Two
Training

The Scout Association
Baden-Powell House
Queen's Gate
London SW7 5JS

First Edition
March 1977
Third Edition
March 1982

Designed by Flavia Malim

Printed in Great Britain by
Eyre & Spottiswoode Ltd
at Grosvenor Press Portsmouth

Introduction

As the recognised National Association in the United Kingdom, The Scout Association is a member of the World Scout Conference. Its own organisation exists by the authority of a Royal Charter, granted by King George V in 1912 and supplemented by further Charters granted by King George VI and Queen Elizabeth II. These Charters give authority to the Bye Laws of the Association, which are approved by Her Majesty's Privy Council. The Bye Laws, in turn, authorise the making of rules for the regulation of the Association's affairs. These have become known as *'Policy, Organisation and Rules'* or, more usually, *'P.O.R.'* and they establish the pattern of the organisation, define its training and provide the skeleton, without which Scouting could not function mechanically, but which is by no means the whole being of the Association.

The Founder called the first set of rules 'Rules for Playing the Game of Scouting', stressing at the outset that it was the practice of good Scouting that was important and not any ponderous collection of regulations which might be interpreted as hampering the man on the spot. Nothing in the Association's attitude has changed over the years. Although they are all integral parts of the Scout Movement every Scout Group is separately registered and has its own individuality. Because of this their structure, operation and standards must be organised and run along common, clearly defined lines. Even so, Scouting is still a game and if other games have rules so that the players know who wins, Scouting needs its rules so that the game can be played well.

Preface

This second part of *Policy, Organisation and Rules* is designed to bring together all the information and requirements concerning the Association's programme of training, together with all details of badges, awards and safety rules.

Rules are numbered here in the same way as in Part One, but do not continue the sequence of those rules. References are given as Rule I, 2 ii, meaning Rule 2 ii in Part One, or Rule II, 5 iii (a), meaning Rule 5 iii (a) in Part 2. Reference to earlier rules in this Part are given as *'See Rule 4 iii above'* and later rules are referred to as *'See Rule II, 5 iii'*.

Since the rules in this Part are concerned entirely with Scout Association policy in training and activities, they apply to all countries in the United Kingdom. However, Northern Ireland and Scotland both have an award which is not given in England and Wales; this is the 'Quest Emblem', for religious knowledge and practice. Details of this award may be obtained from the Northern Ireland or Scottish Headquarters, as appropriate.

Keeping your Rules up to date

Space is provided by a margin on each page, in which the reader should put a mark, together with a note of the number of the page on which the amendment appears. There are numbered pages at the end of the book, left blank for the insertion of amendments. The text of amendments will appear from time to time in *Headquarters Notices* in SCOUTING Magazine.

They will be printed to a style and size to conform with the lay-out of this book so that they can be cut out from the Magazine and pasted in. In reprints of this edition, amended rules will be marked in the margin by an asterisk together with the number of the page at the end of the book on which the amendment will be printed. In new editions, rules will be brought up to date and the pages at the end of the book will again appear blank, for use when incorporating further amendments.

Aim and Method

The Aim of The Scout Association is to encourage the physical, mental and spiritual development of young people so that they may take a constructive place in society. The Method of achieving the Aim of the Association is by providing an enjoyable and attractive scheme of progressive training, based on the Scout Promise and Law and guided by adult leadership.

Promise and Law

The Scout Promise
On my honour, I promise that I will do my best
to do my duty to God and to the Queen,
to help other people
and to keep the Scout Law.

The Scout Law
1. A Scout is to be trusted.
2. A Scout is loyal.
3. A Scout is friendly and considerate.
4. A Scout is a brother to all Scouts.
5. A Scout has courage in all difficulties.
6. A Scout makes good use of his time and is careful of possessions and property.
7. A Scout has respect for himself and for others.

The Cub Scout Promise
I promise that I will do my best
to do my duty to God and to the Queen,
to help other people
and to keep the Cub Scout Law.

The Cub Scout Law
A Cub Scout always does his best,
thinks of others before himself
and does a good turn every day.

Training

Rule 1

The Religious Policy of the Association

The Scout Association includes members of many different forms of religion. The following policy has received the approval of the heads of the leading religious bodies in the United Kingdom.

Rule 1 i

Every Member of the Association is encouraged to:

>make every effort to progress in his understanding and observance of his promise to do his best to do his duty to God;
>belong to some religious body;
>carry into daily practice what he professes.

Rule 1 ii

If a Cub Scout, Scout or Venture Scout does not belong to a religious body, the Scouter responsible for his training must endeavour to put him in touch with one, which should, if possible, be that to which his parents belong or into which he may, in the past, have been formally admitted; the approval of the parents must be obtained.

Rule 1 iii

If a Sponsored (Closed) Group *(See Rule I, 4 iii)* is restricted to members of one particular form of religion or denomination, the Sponsoring

Authority is responsible for the religious training of all the Cub Scouts, Scouts and Venture Scouts in the Group and it is the duty of the Group Scout Leader to encourage attendance at such religious instruction and observances as the Sponsoring Authority may consider desirable.

Rule 1 iv

If a Group is composed of members of several denominations or religions, the Cub Scouts, Scouts and Venture Scouts should be encouraged to attend services of their own form of religion. Any form of daily prayer or divine service in camp should be of the simplest character, attendance being entirely voluntary.

Rule 1 v

The attendance of members of various forms of religion at combined services of a formal character is allowed, provided that the District Commissioner and the religious authorities concerned have given their permission. Attendance at such services must be voluntary.

Rule 1 vi

Scouts' Own Services may be held for the worship of God and to promote a fuller understanding of the significance of the Scout Promise and Law. Such services should be regarded as being supplementary to rather than a substitute for formal attendance at the services of the individual's own form of religion.

Rule 1 vii

If a Cub Scout, Scout or Venture Scout is not allowed, by reasons of his own religious obligations, to attend religious observances of other forms of religion, the Group Scout Leader must make certain that this fact is known by all Leaders concerned, so that they may ensure that the individual's obligations are not compromised while he is under their control.

Rule 1 viii   Chaplains

Chaplains may be appointed as Advisers in Scout Groups, Districts and Counties. Scout Groups may appoint a Chaplain who may be a Minister of Religion or a Layman. In a Scout Group Sponsored by a Church the Priest or Minister may be appointed Group Chaplain. District and County Chaplains may be appointed representing the Church of England, the Church of Scotland, the Church of Ireland, the Presbyterian Church in Ireland, the Church in Wales, the Roman Catholic Church, the Free Churches and the Salvation Army. Their functions include:

(a) Keeping the Group Scout Leader, District Commissioner or County Commissioner informed of the policy of their Churches towards youth work in general and Scouting in particular;

(b) Maintaining close liaison with any Area Youth Chaplains or Committee which may be appointed by their Church Authorities or any Religious Advisory Board or Panel appointed by the appropriate Scout Council;

(c) Advising the Group Scout Leader, District Commissioner or County Commissioner on any matters of Religious Policy or training that might be referred to them.

The Cub Scout Training Programme

Rule 2 — The Cub Scout Training Programme

Rule 2 i   The Cub Scout Badge

On entry into the Cub Scout Pack, a boy begins to work on the requirements for the Cub Scout Badge. This badge takes the form of the World Membership Badge, which the boy is entitled to wear once he is invested as a Member of the Association. The Cub Scout Badge is passed under arrangements made by the Cub Scout Leader. Details of the requirements for this badge appear on Page 19.

Rule 2 ii   The Cub Scout Progress Badges

The Cub Scout Progress Scheme is made up of three Arrow emblems which the Cub Scout gains by taking part in activities from four sections. He gains the Bronze Arrow when he takes part successfully in the first activity and a further two from each section. He gains the Silver Arrow when he takes part successfully in a further three activities from each section. The Gold Arrow is gained when he takes part successfully in three more activities from each section.

The Cub Scout Leader needs to plan programmes involving activities in the Progress Scheme. It is the Cub Scout Leader's responsibility to plan and record the progress of each Cub Scout.

Rule 3 — Cub Scout Proficiency Badges

Rule 3 i

While taking part in activities for the Progress Badges, a boy may also gain proficiency badges as listed under *Cub Scout Training Badges and Emblems* on Pages 19–46. These badges are designed to encourage a boy to develop further individual skills and interests.

Rule 3 ii

Cub Scout Proficiency Badges are gained under arrangements made with suitably competent people by the Cub Scout Leader in consultation with the Group Scout Leader. The District Executive Committee may appoint examiners to supplement Pack arrangements.

Rule 4 — The Link Badge

Rule 4 i

The Link Badge may be gained after a boy has reached the age of ten and a half years. It provides a link between the Cub Scout Pack and the Scout Troop.

Note: A Cub Scout working for, or holding the Link Badge, may take part in a camp with Scouts, provided that the camp is under adult leadership or is at a permanent camp site under adult supervision.

Rule 4 ii
The Link Badge is passed under arrangements made by the Cub Scout Leader. The requirements for the Link Badge appear on Page 47.

Rule 5   Cub Scout Training

Rule 5 i
Details of the structure of the Cub Scout Pack are given in *Rule I, 7 ii*. Details of the appointment and responsibilities of Leaders, Cub Scout Instructors and Instructors, are given in *Rules I, 10, 11, 13 ii and 13 iv*. Minimum standards for Cub Scout Packs are defined in *Rule I, 7 ii (f)*.

Rule 5 ii   Planning
Cub Scout Leaders are responsible for planning programmes of activities for the Cub Scout Pack. The programme should aim to involve interest, adventure and imagination and should help to develop a spirit of co-operation. Attention is drawn to the requirements of safety and to the conditions governing Cub Scout activities in *Activity Rules* on Pages 210–248.

Rule 5 iii   Joint Training
The joint training of Cub Scouts and Brownie Guides may be authorised by the District Commissioner and the appropriate Guide Commissioner in special circumstances such as in a school or village. Such Cub Scout Packs and Brownie Guide Packs must be registered separately with their respective Associations and the Cub Scout Leader must be a woman who also holds a Warrant for the appropriate appointment issued by The Girl Guides Association.

Cub Scout Training Badges and Emblems

The Cub Scout Badge

To be passed under arrangements made by the Cub Scout Leader.
The Arrowhead Badge on a purple background surrounded by a rope in a circle, tied in a reef knot at the bottom.

Requirements

1. Be told the first Jungle Story and how Cub Scouting began.
2. Know the Grand Howl.
3. Know the Scout salute and sign, handshake and motto.
4. Know the Cub Scout Promise and Law.

The Cub Scout Progress Badges

The Bronze Arrow

A bronze arrow on a green background.

The Silver Arrow

A silver arrow on a green background.

The Gold Arrow

A gold arrow on a green background.

The Cub Scout Leader is responsible for planning and recording activities undertaken by the Cub Scout. Arrangements for the assessment of success are made by the Cub Scout Leader.

The Cub Scout takes part successfully in activities selected from the following four sections: Growing Up, Discovering, Thinking and Sharing.

The Cub Scout gains the Bronze Arrow when he takes part successfully in the first activity and a further two from each section. He gains the Silver Arrow when he takes part successfully in a further three activities from each section. The Gold Arrow is gained when he takes part successfully in three more activities from each section.

Growing Up
. . . to be fit and able to take care of yourself

1 **Lay a trail of tracking signs and follow a trail laid by someone else.**
2 Practise so that you can take part successfully in a game involving ball throwing and catching.
3 Practise any three sports training activities, such as skipping, balancing, somersault, leapfrog, etc.
4 Go for a walk with an older person and explain how to use the *Green Cross Code.*
5 Improve your memory with observation games.
6 Climb up a tree or rope.
7 Make your own bed and find out how to make your bed in camp.
8 Cook a simple meal indoors.
9 Learn to swim. Discuss the water safety rules with other Cub Scouts or a Leader.
10 Ride a bicycle safely.
11 Pack your kit after playing football or going

swimming, or unpack and put away your kit after returning from a holiday.

12 Know how to apply simple first aid and how and when to get adult help.

13 Play in a team for at least four matches.

14 Go on an expedition of at least five kilometres with a Scout or an adult.

15 Take part in an emergency drill and know what to do in case of a fire.

16 Help to pitch a tent.

17 Explain to a leader how to keep yourself fit and the dangers of damaging your health.

18 Use a compass to find your way to a secret destination.

19 Swim 100 metres. Discuss the water safety rules with other Cub Scouts or a Leader.

20 Go on an obstacle course, including such things as a monkey bridge, rope swing, climbing net, etc.

21 Make a first aid kit and know how to use the contents. Take it with you on an outing.

22 Light a fire out-of-doors and cook something on it.

23 With a grown-up try a new sport, such as roller-skating, ski-ing, judo, fishing, horse riding, sailing, canoeing, trampolining, etc.

24 Help to build a tree house.

25 Learn how to tie your tie and your shoelaces. Other activities may be undertaken at the discretion of the Cub Scout Leader. Guidance on activities and programmes can be found in *The Cub Scout Leader's Handbook*.

Discovering
. . . new skills and interests

1 **Use two of the following in an activity: reef knot, clove hitch, round turn and two half hitches, bowline, highwayman's hitch, hank a short rope.**

2 Find out about the three crosses of the Union Flag and learn the National Anthem.

Know what to do when flags are flown and national anthems played.

3 Make something from odds and ends.

4 Find out something new about any animal, tree, fish, bird or plant which you see on an expedition.

5 Discover something of interest about the Royal Family, such as types of transport they use, their hobbies, places they visit, etc.

6 Grow a plant in a garden or a plant pot.

7 Draw or paint a picture of any subject of your choice.

8 Think up and use a secret code.

9 Take care of a pet for at least a week.

10 Make and fly a kite.

11 Make a puppet and take part in a puppet play.

12 Provide the birds with food and water regularly.

13 Watch three different types of machinery at work, such as a crane, caterpillar-tracked vehicle, combine harvester, earth mover, tractor, fishing boat gear, etc. Explain to a Leader the work they do.

14 Play at least three tunes on a recorder, guitar or other instrument.

15 Find out something about exploration, for example in space, underwater or underground.

16 Make something out of wood, metal or other material using the correct tools.

17 Help an adult with the routine maintenance of a bicycle or other machinery like a model railway, sewing machine or a car.

18 Carry out three scientific experiments.

19 Make up a story of about 100 words and tell it to your Pack.

20 Collect five foreign coins. Explain how much they are worth and explain the symbols on them.

21 Construct a working model such as a draw-bridge, a conveyor belt, a windmill, etc.
22 Make a plaster cast of an animal's or bird's footprint. Discuss its way of life with other Cub Scouts or a Leader.
23 Find out more about Baden-Powell and how Scouting began.
24 Find out the emblems of three airlines and the types of aircraft they use. Explain why airlines use the 24-hour clock.

Other activities may be undertaken at the discretion of the Cub Scout Leader. Guidance on activities and programmes can be found in *The Cub Scout Leader's Handbook*.

Thinking
. . . about ourselves and others

1 **Keep a diary of good turns for a week, showing how you have helped other people.**
2 Draw, act or tell the story of someone whose job it is to 'help other people'.
3 Offer to do two good turns at home – and do them.
4 Visit an old people's home, children's home or hospital ward and help to do something useful, as a Pack or Six.
5 Make a 'Thank You' card or write a letter and send it to someone on behalf of the Pack.
6 Find out about someone who has 'done their best' in the past. Act or mime the story.
7 Explain some of the country's laws about litter, why these laws are made and how you can help to keep them.
8 Assist at a Service at your own place of worship.
9 Look at five different advertisements on television or in magazine and explain which

you think does the best job.

10 Take part in a Pack Meeting about Cub Scouts in another country – the games they play, their activities, their language and food.

11 Help a newcomer to settle in at your school or Pack.

12 Write some prayers for use by your Pack.

13 Find out something about life in your area in the past and act any special events or describe any interesting buildings.

14 Explain to a Leader the meaning or reason for different Services in your Church, Chapel or wherever you worship.

15 Learn to speak five useful phrases in another language.

16 Carry out a survey of boy's clothes, find out what your friends think about them and what they like wearing best.

17 Make a poster to advertise Cub Scouting to younger boys.

18 Find out something about three different forms of communication, such as radio, television, semaphore, smoke signals, drums, newspapers, telephone, etc.

19 Keep an account of how you have spent your pocket-money for a fortnight, showing what you have spent on sweets, clothes, presents or other things, and how much you have saved.

20 Help to plan and carry out a conservation project.

21 Help to organise and take part in an act of worship for the Pack.

22 Invite a nurse, doctor, fireman, clergyman, policeman or social worker to your Pack Meeting to talk about their work. Then discuss with your friends how you could help them.

23 Find out something about two forms of worship which are different from your own.

24 Help to welcome visitors to your Pack Meeting and make them feel at home.

Other activities may be undertaken at the discretion of the Cub Scout Leader. Guidance on activities and programmes can be found in *The Cub Scout Leader's Handbook*.

Sharing

. . . our thoughts and experiences with others

1 **By acting a playlet with your Six or with a friend, show how accidents in the home can be prevented.**

2 Find out the meaning of the badges which were given to you, when you were invested. Fold your scarf properly and find out why you wear it.

3 Draw five traffic signs or symbols and know what they mean.

4 With a friend, make use of two of the following – an adventure playground, a library, museum, art gallery, leisure centre, swimming pool or supermarket.

5 Use a public telephone and a private telephone.

6 Invent a 'car passenger code' of behaviour and some travel games.

7 Go on a Pack Holiday, spending at least a night away from home.

8 Walk around your local area following a sketch map; mark on it the position of your home and other important places such as your school, Church, Pack meeting place, park, shops, garage, bus stop, telephone kiosk, etc.

9 Arrange to invite a friend or two to your home for a meal which you have helped to plan, cook and serve. Clear up afterwards.

10 On a Pack outdoor activity show that you know the *Country Code* and the reasons for it.

11 Visit a railway or bus station and learn how to use the timetable.

12 Help your family to plan and go on an expedition. Tell a leader about it afterwards.

13 Offer to do three different jobs for a person such as a farmer, postman, policeman, forester, fisherman, roadman, district nurse, etc., and do them. Tell the Pack about it.

14 Show a friend around a place of interest.

15 Make a chart of all the people who help to run your school, showing the different kinds of work they do. List the ways you can help your school.

16 Go on an expedition to a place such as a fire station, farm, newspaper printing works, telephone exchange, rubbish disposal plant, a radio station, television centre, lifeboat station, etc. Discuss how they help the community with other Cub Scouts or a Leader.

17 Using a map, help to plan a route for your summer holiday or a Pack expedition.

18 Go on a Cub Camp, spending at least a night under canvas.

19 Make your own weather station with at least two instruments. Keep a log over a period of a fortnight (charts, comments, drawings, etc.).

20 Describe to a Leader three different television programmes you have seen in a week.

21 Help the Pack Leaders to plan and run an outing.

22 Help another Cub Scout to do something he finds difficult.

23 Take part in a play, concert or Group show.

Other activities may be undertaken at the discretion of the Cub Scout Leader. Guidance or activities and programmes can be found in *The Cub Scout Leader's Handbook*.

Cub Scout Proficiency Badges

Cub Scout Proficiency Badges are passed under arrangements made by the Cub Scout Leader, in consultation with the Group Scout Leader. They have a red background, except for the Athlete and Swimmer Badges, which have a red, yellow or green background, indicating stages of achievement attained in that order. Collective Achievement Badges are circular, and are gained by a group of boys working together. The World Conservation Badge has a brown background.

Animal Lover

Requirements

Choose any two of the following alternatives:

1. Keep a scrapbook and tell the examiner about any six animals you have seen (not native ones), their countries of origin, feeding habits and details of the special care they need.

2. Look after a pet for at least three months. Keep a record of its feeding habits and how you have looked after it. Know how to recognise common illnesses and what special care is needed before and after the birth of young animals.

3. Help to care for a farm animal for a season. Keep a record of its feeding habits and the kind of work you have done. Know how to recognise common illnesses and what special care is needed before and after the birth of young farm animals.

4. Belong to an animal or bird society. *Either* take part in one of its activities *or* make progress in any award scheme offered.

5. Keep a record (e.g. in pictures, sketches,

photographs or on tape), for one month of bird, animal and/or insect life in your garden or specific area in a park or farm.

6. Find out about one of the following: bird life; butterflies, moths or other insects; native wild animals; friends and enemies of the garden; seashore, pond or river life.

Artist

Requirements

Choose any three of the following alternatives, at least one of which is to be done in the presence of the examiner:

1. Draw, with a pencil, brush, pen or crayon, an original illustration of any incident, character or scene. Size not less than 18 × 13 cm (7 × 5 inches).

2. Design and make a greetings card.

3. Make a model in clay or other plastic material. Size not less than 10 cm (4 inches) square.

4. Make a decorative article from cane, raffia, wool, leather, wood or any other suitable material approved in advance by the examiner.

5. Make a design and print it on paper or fabric (e.g. using potato cuts or lino cuts).

6. Make a worthwhile toy or model of a reasonable size.

7. Undertake a project, having agreed it with the examiner, involving the use of a plastic or metal construction kit. The standard expected should demand an imaginative approach and a high quality of workmanship.

Athlete

(A three stage badge)

Requirements

There are three stages in this badge. When you reach the standards for any of the three stages you wear a badge as follows:

Stage 1 – red background;
Stage 2 – yellow background;
Stage 3 – green background;

Badges for successive stages may be worn simultaneously.

You must gain the following points from four previously chosen events: 22 points for Stage 1; 30 points for Stage 2; 35 points for Stage 3.

1. 50 metres Sprint

10 points	*7 points*	*5 points*
9 seconds	10 seconds	11 seconds

2. Throwing the Cricket Ball – using a 135 gm (4¾ oz) ball

10 points	*7 points*	*5 points*
30 metres	24 metres	18 metres
(100′)	(80′)	(60′)

3. High Jump

10 points	*7 points*	*5 points*
0.96 metres	0.86 metres	0.76 metres
(3′ 2″)	(2′ 10″)	(2′ 6″)

4. Long Jump

10 points	*7 points*	*5 points*
3 metres	2.5 metres	2 metres
(10′)	(8′)	(6′ 6″)

5. 400 metre Run

10 points	*7 points*	*5 points*
90 seconds	100 seconds	110 seconds

6. Sargent Jump – measurements refer to height on target

10 points	7 points	5 points
35 cm	30 cm	25 cm
(14″)	(12″)	(10″)

Note: When Requirement No 3 is undertaken, special regard must be given to the nature of the jump and the landing facilities required. Unless expert tuition and supervision is available the Fosbury Flop should not *be attempted.*

Book Reader

Requirements

1. Produce a list of books you have read recently, name their authors and be able to tell the examiner something about three of the books. The three books to be chosen by you are to include at least one story and at least one factual book.

Note: The three books must be of a reasonable standard, taking the Cub Scout's age and development into account.

2. Show that you understand how to care for books.

3. Show that you can use a dictionary, encyclopaedia and an atlas.

4. Explain to the examiner how the books in a library are set out and how you would find a specific fiction book.

Camper
(Collective Achievement)

Requirements

Carry out the following as a member of a group of boys and not by yourself. This group could be your Pack or Six.

1. Camp overnight under canvas on two separate occasions.
2. Pack your own kit for a weekend camp.
3. Help to pitch and strike a tent.
4. Know how to care for a tent at camp.
5. Make a simple camp gadget.
6. At camp help to prepare, cook, serve and clear away a simple meal.
7. Know the basic health and safety rules for camp.
8. Help to tidy up the camp site before you leave.

Note: This badge should only be approached with adequate and proper preparation and supervision, including reference to Rules II, 71 and 73.

Collector

Requirements

1. Make a collection of a number of similar items (e.g. stamps, postcards, matchboxes or fossils).
2. Arrange your collection neatly and systematically, labelling items correctly and clearly.
3. Talk about items in your collection that particularly interest you.
4. Visit a collection made by someone else and explain what you like or dislike about the presentation of the collection, choice of venue, etc. This could be a personal or public collection.

Communicator

Requirements

1. Demonstrate how to use the telephone and know how to make an emergency call.

2. Write a formal letter (e.g. thanking a visitor to your Pack).

3. Choose any three of the following alternatives:

(a) Send and receive three short messages using signals (e.g. Morse Code, semaphore).

(b) Make a verbal report of a local event either past or present.

(c) Write and decipher three simple messages in code.

(d) Hold a simple conversation in another language.

(e) Make and maintain a link with another Cub Scout Pack through tapes, letters, etc.

(f) Hold a simple conversation without talking (e.g. by manual alphabet or understand and read a piece of Braille writing).

(g) Memorise a message and deliver it twenty minutes later.

Cook

Requirements

1. Plan, cook, serve and clear away a two course meal for at least two people. The following dishes are given as suggestions. You may produce your own menu which will be approved by the examiner beforehand.

Main Courses

    Shepherds Pie

    Egg Salad

    Sausage Rolls

    Cauliflower Cheese

    Fish Pie

Puddings

    Baked Apple with custard
    Fruit Crumble
    Eve's Pudding
    Jelly Whip/Trifle
    Suet Roly-Poly

2. Know how to prepare and cook fresh vegetables.

3. Make either scones, small cakes, biscuits or tarts.

4. Make and serve a hot drink.

5. Know the basic rules of safety and hygiene in the kitchen and the reasons for them.

Cyclist

Requirements

1. Own or have the regular use of a bicycle of proper size.

2. Be able to mount and dismount properly.

3. Be able to clean and oil a bicycle and pump up the tyres.

4. Understand the need for keeping the bicycle in a road-worthy condition, and help to do this.

5. Understand the need for keeping a bicycle locked when leaving it unattended.

6. Know how, and help, to mend a puncture.

7. Under observation go for a short ride on a specified course, showing a knowledge of the proper use of those signals and rules applicable to cyclists as set out in the *Highway Code* in the section for the Road User on Wheels and Extra Rules for Cyclists. (The route shall, if possible, include a cross-roads, pedestrian crossing, right-hand turn and roundabout.)

Note: A Cub Scout who has passed the National Cycling Proficiency Test of the Royal Society for the Prevention of Accidents qualifies automatically for parts 2, 3 and 4 of this badge. The National Cycling Proficiency Test will only qualify for part 7 if it included a test on the highway.

Entertainer
(Collective Achievement)

Requirements

Carry out two of the following as a member of a group of boys and not by yourself. This group could be your Pack or Six.

1. Create a play and perform it.

2. Make puppets for, and produce, a puppet play or shadowgraph.

3. Produce a recorded show (e.g. for someone who is housebound).

4. Sing a programme of songs, carols or hymns.

5. Perform some folk dancing.

6. Make a selection of simple rhythm instruments and use them as an accompaniment to songs.

7. Perform a display of tumbling tricks.

8. Make up and produce short dances to pieces of music of your own choice.

9. Take an active part in a Pack band or Gang Show.

Note: Other forms of entertainment of comparable standard are acceptable if they are agreed with the examiner beforehand.

Explorer
(Collective Achievement)

Requirements

Carry out the following as a member of a group of boys and not by yourself. This group could be your Pack or Six.

1. Discuss with the examiner the preparations required for a one day expedition in the countryside, e.g. cost of expedition, correct clothing, footwear, first aid kit and food.

2. Take part in two Cub Scout expeditions, one of which must be entirely out of doors.

3. Build a simple shelter.

4. Build and light a fire outdoors and then make a hot drink.

5. Find your way to a place in town or countryside, 1 kilometre (half a mile) away, by following directions given to you by the examiner (either compass directions or signs made on the ground, or landmarks, or a combination of these).

First Aider

Requirements

1. Know the limits of first aid and the need for getting adult help.

2. Know how to control bleeding by direct pressure on a wound.

3. Know the importance of cleanliness and show how to dress minor cuts and grazes with gauze and roller bandages; apply and remove adhesive dressings.

4. Demonstrate the use of a triangular bandage as a large arm sling and a knee bandage.

5. Demonstrate how to make a patient comfortable.

6. Know the common causes of burns and scalds in the home and their prevention; how to put out burning clothing; the simple treatment of burns and scalds.

7. Have a knowledge of the mouth-to-mouth method of respiratory resuscitation and where possible demonstrate this method by use of a manikin or approved aid.

Fisherman

Requirements

1. Hold the Swimmer Badge (Stage 1).

2. Know the dates of the closed seasons and the minimum sizes of fish which may be retained for the areas in which you fish.

3. (a) Know how to remove a hook from a fish's mouth without damaging the fish and how to kill the fish properly.

(b) Recognise six different fish from photographs. Know the best baits to use for any four fish, the places in which they lie and the best way to fish for them.

4. Keep a log book over a period of three months of fishing trips undertaken. The log to contain a note of water conditions, weather, wind direction and strength, species and numbers of fish caught and baits which prove successful.

Gardener

Requirements

1. *Either* look after a patch of garden for at least three months. Know what tools are needed and how to use and look after them. Grow something in your garden suitable for the time of year.

Or grow a variety of plants indoors and know the conditions under which they must be kept.

2. Choose any two of the following alternatives:

(a) Grow vegetables or flowers from seed; know how to prick out and transplant.

(b) Know about hazards to plants and flowers (e.g. diseases, pests) and understand what preventative measures can be taken and what can be done to aid growth.

(c) Find out about one of the following: tree

and shrubs; wild flowers; friends and enemies of the garden; ferns and grasses or other plant life.

(d) Either know how to store vegetables and how long they may be stored, or show how to prepare flowers for display to give maximum effect.

Handyman

Requirements

1. Know what to do in the event of a burst water pipe or gas leak and know what to do in an electricity power cut and how to turn off the electricity supply at home.

2. Know the colour code of electric plug wiring and demonstrate how to change a plug.

3. Know what to do in the case of fire.

4. Make a useful article for use in the Pack Den or at home.

5. Demonstrate the use of and how to take care of the following tools: hammer, saw, screwdriver, spanner, pliers.

6. Make and put in a suitable position a nesting box or bird table.

7. Demonstrate how to prepare and paint a vertical surface and clean a paint brush.

Hobbies

Requirements

Show a continuing interest and progress, over a period of at least three months, in a hobby or skill; be able to demonstrate it and/or discuss it with the examiner.

Note: Suitable hobbies might be collecting, chess, singing in a choir, etc. A Cub Scout may gain and wear any number of Hobbies Badges subject to his pursuing each hobby for three months.

Home Help

Requirements

1. Fry bacon or sausages; boil, fry or poach an egg; prepare and cook potatoes.

2. Lay a table and serve a simple meal. (This can be done in conjunction with 1 above.)

3. Wash up afterwards and show how to deal with a saucepan, cutlery, glassware, etc.

4. Wash and iron your Group scarf.

5. Sew on a badge or button.

6. Make a bed.

7. Clean windows, and silver or brasswork.

8. Clean and tidy a room.

Map Reader

Requirements

1. Know the principal signs used on a 1:50 000 scale O.S. map of your locality. Be able to pin-point your home and Pack Den. Explain how well-known local features of your choice are represented on the map.

2. Make a scale model of an 80 metres (250 ft) hill – showing the contour layers at regular intervals.

3. Understand all of paras. 1 and 2 so that you can describe what you would see along a 5 kilometre (3-mile) stretch of road set by the examiner on any 1:50 000 scale map.

4. Set a map and know how to use a compass.

Musician

Requirements

1. Explain the major symbols on a musical score and give the correct meaning of common musical terms.

2. Sing two songs or play two pieces of your own choice which show different styles and tempos.

3. Choose any two of the following alternatives:

(a) Sight read a simple piece set by the examiner.

(b) Demonstrate some musical exercises which improve your playing or singing.

(c) Name the parts of your instrument or know how your voice works.

(d) Know how to look after your instrument or voice.

(e) Know the storyline of an opera, ballet or folk song.

(f) Clap out the rhythm of a piece played by the examiner.

Photographer

Requirements

1. Take a set of twelve pictures or 2½ minutes of movie film describing an event or outing. These should be of varied subjects (e.g. landscapes, people and action shots) and may be in colour or black and white, and home or commercially processed. N.B. All twelve pictures or movie film need not necessarily be taken on the one occasion.

2. Discuss with the examiner the main features of a camera (i.e. shutter speeds, lens focusing and apertures) and films. Explain how they are used to ensure technically good results. If you have an "instant" camera explain how the film is instantly developed and demonstrate how to load the camera.

3. By mounting the prints or projecting the transparencies, use them to describe to other Cub Scouts the outing or event mentioned in paragraph 1.

Rescuer

Requirements

1. Hold the Swimmer Badge (Stage 3).

2. (a) Understand and where possible demonstrate the following methods of rescue – reach, throw, wade and row.

(b) Enter the water, swim 25 metres to the subject. Tow for 25 metres, using a towing aid, e.g. lifebuoy, piece of wood, etc., and on completion of the tow secure the subject in the support position.

(c) Jump or dive into the water, surface and swim 10 metres. Recover an object 2.5–4.5 kilogrammes (5–10 lbs.) from a depth of at least 1.2 metres (4 feet). Bring to the starting point using life-saving backstroke.

(These tests need only be done in swimwear.)

3. Using a training manikin where possible demonstrate the expired air (mouth-to-mouth) method of respiratory resuscitation.

4. Answer four questions on water safety.

5. Show methods of rescue, and the precautions to be taken in the case of ice-breaking and an outbreak of fire indoors.

Note: A Cub Scout who has gained the Elementary Award of the Royal Life Saving Society qualifies automatically for parts 2, 3 and 4.

Scientist

Requirements

Choose two experiments from each section of the badge and explain to and/or show the examiner what you have done. Where appropriate explain any conclusions you have made.

The Home

1. Connect up simple circuits with bulbs, batteries and switches.

2. Demonstrate that electrical current produced magnetic, chemical and heating effects.

3. Find out what happens when you mix lemon juice and baking powder.

4. Make an invisible ink from a household substance.

5. Make some yoghourt and find out how living creatures are involved in the process.

6. Find out how well your house is insulated (for example, the loft, water pipes, water tank, cavity wall); suggest how the amount of insulation could be increased to advantage.

The Physical World

1. Make an artificial rainbow by splitting up a beam of white light.

2. Make a pin-hole camera.

3. Keep simple weather records over a month (e.g. rainfall, temperature, cloud cover, wind direction).

4. Make a simple periscope.

5. Make a telephone using string to transmit the sound.

6. Demonstrate how to recover dissolved substances from sea water or river water.

The Living World

1. Grow cress (or a similar plant) and investigate what happens when light and water are excluded from it.

2. Use a net and jar to find out how many different creatures live in the water and mud at the edge of a pond.

3. Set up a wormery or ant colony and record activity over a few weeks.

4. Grow a bean or pea and keep a record of its growth.

5. Grow a bean or pea. When the root and shoot are visible investigate what happens when the seed is turned upside-down and left to continue growing.

6. Collect seeds from various plants and

discover how these are protected and dispersed.
7. Investigate what happens to your pulse rate before and after exercise.

Note: Other experiments of a comparable standard are acceptable if agreed with the examiner beforehand.

Sportsman

Requirements

1. Have a broad knowledge of two sports such as Rugby Football, Association Football, Cricket, Hockey, Rounders, Horse Riding, Judo, Archery.

2. Show reasonable proficiency and be taking an active part regularly in at least one of these.

3. Show that you know how to look after the equipment and clothing necessary for the game selected to pass part 2: e.g. blow up a football and take care of your football boots, take care of your cricket bat and know how to look after cricket pads.

4. Show a good sportsmanlike spirit in all Cub Scout games and activities.

5. Know the importance of taking a shower or bath after games if possible, or at least changing out of the clothes worn during the game. Know also the importance of good care of the feet.

Note: Certificates must be produced for part 2 from the Cub Scout Leader or a school teacher and for part 4 from the Cub Scout Leader.

Swimmer

(A three stage badge)

Requirements

There are three stages in this badge. When you reach the standards for any of the three stages you wear a badge as follows:

Stage 1 – red background
Stage 2 – yellow background
Stage 3 – green background

Badges for successive stages may be worn simultaneously.

Stage 1

Perform the following:

1. A jump or dive from the side of the bath.
2. Breathing exercise.
3. Front glide.
4. Back glide.
5. Front paddle 10 metres.
6. Back paddle 10 metres.
7. Backstroke, without use of arms, hands on hips, 10 metres.
8. 25 metres of either breast-stroke, front crawl or back crawl.

Note: A Cub Scout who holds the Swimming Teachers' Association "Junior Swimmer Badge" qualifies automatically for a Stage 1 Swimmer Badge.

Stage 2

Requirements 1 to 4 to be performed in shirt and shorts or pyjamas.

Perform the following:

1. Tread water for 1 minute in a vertical position.
2. A surface dive to touch the bottom with both hands in at least shoulder depth water.
3. Mushroom float for 5 seconds.
4. Swim across the width of the bath on any front stroke. At the halfway mark turn over

on to the back and finish the distance on any back stroke of your choice.

5. Remove clothing whilst in the water, without touching the bottom or side of the bath.

6. Plunge (dive and glide) as far as possible.

7. Commencing with the appropriate racing start, swim 25 metres front or back crawl.

8. Commencing with the appropriate racing start, swim 25 metres breast or butterfly stroke.

Note: A Cub Scout who holds the Swimming Teachers' Association "Cadet Badge" qualifies automatically for a Stage 2 Swimmer Badge.

Stage 3

Perform the following, in the order set out, without a break:

1. Dressed in trousers and shirt or pyjamas, effect an entry from the side of the bath by a straddle or a tuck jump.

2. Swim 45 metres.

3. Tread water for 3 minutes in a vertical position.

4. Undress in the water.

5. Swim 400 metres, surface diving once during the swim, and swimming at least 5 metres completely submerged.

6. Climb out from deep water without the use of steps or assistance.

Note: A Cub Scout who has qualified for the Bronze Personal Survival Award of the Amateur Swimming Association qualifies automatically for a Stage 3 Swimmer Badge.

World Conservation

(Collective Achievement)

Requirements

Carry out the following as a member of a group of boys and not by yourself. This group could be your Pack or Six.

1. Take part as a group in two projects, such as:

(a) clearing a ditch, pond or creek;

(b) making, setting up and maintaining a bird feeder, bird table, bird nesting box or bird bath;

(c) creating, cultivating and maintaining a garden and a compost heap;

(d) a nature survey;

(e) an anti-litter campaign;

(f) planting a buddleia bush and keeping a record of the 'visitors' to it;

(g) making a footpath map of an area from your own investigation.

Note: Other projects may be undertaken as agreed by the Cub Scout Leader.

2. Go on an expedition with your group into the countryside and:

(a) find some examples showing how man has damaged nature and other examples showing how man has improved nature;

(b) know the *Country Code*, know the reasons for the *Country Code*, and show that you are doing your best to keep it.

3. Carry out the following:

(a) find out all you can about an animal, bird, plant, fish, etc., which is in danger of extinction in your own country; find out what can be done to save it and, if possible, help to do so with expert advice;

(b) find out which creatures and plants are in the greatest danger of extinction in the world and what can be done to save them; find out if you can personally do anything to help save them;

(c) do what you can to inform other people by, for example:

    (i) making posters or a display;

    (ii) talking to adults (e.g. at a Parents' Evening);

    (iii) talking to other young people.

4. With your group find out about one of the processes of nature, for example:

(a) observe either how a plant grows, a butterfly or frog develops, or some similar process of nature; report on your observations, either using a wall chart, log book, photographs or drawings;

(b) visit a zoo or natural history museum, and make a scrapbook about the feeding habits of one of the animals or birds;

(c) carry out an experiment which shows the effects of pollution in water or in the air and make a chart or display of your findings;

(d) observe and record the effect of the processes of nature in action on a stretch of coastline.

Note: Other projects may be undertaken as agreed by the Cub Scout Leader.

5. Improve your environment by:

(a) planting a tree or shrub;

(b) grassing an area where there is no vegetation cover;

or:

(c) growing plants in a window box or indoors.

Note: Where Cub Scouts are encouraged to carry out a project anywhere near water, for example clearing a ditch or pond or carrying out a small fish survey, leaders must make adequate arrangements for the safety of Cub Scouts and ensure that the activity is properly supervised.

The Link Badge

To be passed under arrangements made by the Cub Scout Leader.

Three gold links on a green background.

Requirements

1. Be at least ten and a half years old.

2. Visit your Scout Leader and register for entry into the Troop before going up.

3. Take part in a Patrol activity out of doors.

4. Show general knowledge of the Scout Movement and the development of world-wide Scouting.

5. Know the Scout Promise and Law and discuss their meaning with your future Scout Leader.

Service Stars

Awarded by the Cub Scout Leader.

Requirements

Service Stars are awarded to Cub Scouts after one, two or three years in the Pack.

The Sixer's Badge

Awarded by the Cub Scout Leader

Two gold bars and the Arrowhead Badge on a green background.

The Second's Badge

Awarded by the Cub Scout Leader and the Sixer.

One gold bar and the Arrowhead Badge on a green background.

Method of Wear

Cub Scout training badges are worn on the uniform as shown in the illustration on Page 265. Other emblems relevant to Cub Scout uniform are detailed in Uniform on Pages 180–185.

The Scout Training Programme

Rule 6 — Entry to the Scout Troop

Boys may enter the Scout Troop either from the Cub Scout Pack, on making the Scout Promise and acquiring the Scout Badge (see page 57) or as new Members of the Association, on making the Scout Promise and acquiring the Scout Badge. The Scout Badge is the same as the World Membership Badge and is passed under arrangements made by the Scout Leader.

Rule 7 — The Patrol System

Rule 7 i

The organisation of the Scout Troop, which is made up of a number of Patrols, each led by a Patrol Leader, forms an essential feature of Scout training, which includes training in leadership and in planning and carrying out activities in the context of self-reliance.

Rule 7 ii

The training of Patrol Leaders and the provision of opportunities for leadership by allowing them full status in the affairs of the Troop, through the Patrol Leaders' Council and by acting as instructors and examiners, is vital to the success of the training.

Rule 7 iii

At camp, Patrols live and work as self-contained units.

Rule 8

Scout Progress Badges

Rule 8 i

The Scout training programme involves the acquisition of three Progress Badges:
The Scout Standard (normally gained within a year of transfer or investiture),
The Advanced Scout Standard (normally gained by a boy's fourteenth birthday),
The Chief Scout's Award.

Rule 8 ii

The requirements of these badges may be met in any order that is convenient to the Scout and it is not necessary for him to meet all the requirements of one before proceeding to the next. However, the Scout Standard must have been gained through meeting all its requirements before the Advanced Scout Standard can be awarded. Similarly, the Advanced Scout Standard must have been gained before the Chief Scout's Award can be awarded.

Rule 8 ii

The Scout Standard is passed under arrangements made by a Patrol Leader and awarded on the recommendation of the Patrol Leaders' Council. The Advanced Scout Standard is passed under arrangements made by the Scout Leader and on the recommendation of the Patrol Leaders' Council. The Chief Scout's Award is passed under arrangements made by the Scout Leader and on the recommendation of the Patrol Leaders' Council.

The requirements for the Scout Progress Badges appear on pages 58–66.

Rule 8 iv

Scout Progress Badges may continue to be worn after the next Progress Badge has been gained, e.g., the Link Badge may still be worn after the Scout Standard has been gained. The positions for wearing these badges are as follows:

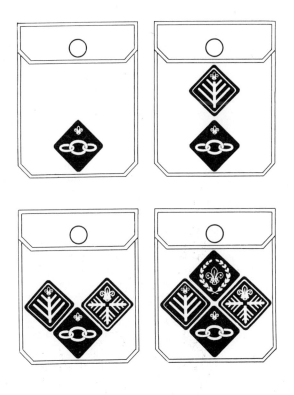

Rule 9

Scout Proficiency Badges

Rule 9 i

While working on the three Progress Badges, a Scout may also gain proficiency badges as listed under Scout Proficiency Badges on pages 67–161. These badges are designed to allow Scouts to demonstrate individual skills and interests and to participate with others in the performance of activities.

Rule 9 ii

Scout Proficiency Badges are in five groups:

Interest – of an elementary nature, open to all Scouts but primarily intended for boys of 12–13 years:

Pursuit – of a practical nature, open to all Scouts but primarily intended for boys of 13–15 years;

Service – involving both theory and practice, open to all Scouts, but primarily intended for older Scouts. The standards of badges in this group may not be varied for younger boys;

Instructor – involving both the theory and practice of instruction, open to all Scouts but primarily intended for older Scouts. Instructor badges may be acquired by those holding the appropriate Interest, Pursuit, Service, Collective Achievement or Air or Sea Training badges. No more than two Instructor badges may be held.

Collective Achievement – to encourage a Scout Patrol or group of Scouts to work together on a project. The standard and duration of the project will be decided by the Patrol Leaders' Council in consultation with those who are attempting to gain the badge.

Rule 9 iii

(a) Scout Proficiency Badges in the Interest, Pursuit and Service Groups and the Sea and Air Training Badges are gained under arrangements made with suitably competent people by the Scout Leader in consultation with the Group Scout Leader. The District Executive Committee may appoint examiners to supplement Troop arrangements.

(b) Badges in the Instructor group are passed under arrangements made by an examiner appointed by the District Executive Committee.

(c) Collective Achievement Badges are awarded by the Patrol Leaders' Council, which will assess the project on the basis of progress, perseverance and achievement by the Patrol or group of Scouts. The requirements for these badges appear on pages 67–161.

Collective Achievement Badges are worn on uniform as shown in the illustration on page 271.

Rule 10 The Venture Scout Membership Badge

A Scout may work and qualify for the Venture Scout Membership Badge and may meet requirements for the Venture Award during the three months immediately prior to his transfer to the Venture Scout Unit *(See Rule I, 7 iii (f))*.

Rule 11

Scout Training

Rule 11 i
Details of the structure of the Scout Troop are given in *Rule I, 7 iii*. Details of the appointment and responsibilities of Leaders and Instructors are given in *Rules I, 10, 11, 13 v and vi*. Minimum standards for Scout Troops are defined in *Rule I, 7 iii (g)*.

Rule 11 ii   Planning
Scout Leaders are responsible for planning programmes of activities for the Scout Troop in consultation with the Patrol Leaders' Council. Activities should include, but not be restricted to, those related to Progress and Proficiency Badges. Attention is drawn to *Activity Rules* on pages 210–248.

Rule 12

The Sea Training Programme

Rule 12 i
The Sea Training Programme establishes the pattern of training for Sea Scouts and provides additional specialised training for all Scouts who may wish to take part in water activities. It is not a substitute for the training followed by other Scouts, and the Scout Progress Badges remain the basis of the training for all Scouts.

Rule 12 ii
The Sea Training Programme is in three stages, followed in parallel with the stages of the Scout Training Programme as shown below:
☐ while working on the Scout Standard, Sea Scouts also work on the Boatman Badge;

□ while working on the Advanced Scout Standard, Sea Scouts also work on the Coxswain's Mate Badge;

□ while working on the Chief Scout's Award, Sea Scouts also work on the Coxswain Badge.

Rule 12 iii

All Scout Proficiency Badges may be acquired by Sea Scouts and all Sea Training Badges may be acquired by all Scouts. If any Scout develops a strong interest in the Sea Training Programme, he should be encouraged to transfer to a Sea Scout Troop if one is available locally.

Rule 12 iv

The Sea Training Badges are gained under arrangements made with suitably competent people by the Scout Leader in consultation with the Group Scout Leader.

Attention is drawn to *Activity Rules* on pages 210–248.

Rule 13

The Air Training Programme

Rule 13 i

The Air Training Programme establishes the pattern of training for Air Scouts and provides additional specialised training for all Scouts who may wish to take part in air activities. It is not a substitute for the training followed by other Scouts, and the Scout Progress Badges remain the basis for the training of all Scouts.

Rule 13 ii

The Air Training Programme is in three stages, followed in parallel with the stages of the Scout

Training Programme as shown below:

- □ while working on the Scout Standard, Air Scouts also work on the Airman Badge;
- □ while working on the Advanced Scout Standard, Air Scouts also work on the Senior Airman Badge;
- □ while working on the Chief Scout's Award, Air Scouts also work on the Master Airman Badge.

Rule 13 iii

All Scout Proficiency Badges may be acquired by Air Scouts and all Air Training Badges may be acquired by all Scouts. If any Scout develops a strong interest in the Air Training Programme, he should be encouraged to transfer to an Air Scout Troop if one is available locally.

Rule 13 iv

The Air Training Badges are gained under arrangements made with suitably competent people by the Scout Leader in consultation with the Group Scout Leader.

Attention is drawn to *Activity Rules* on pages 210–248.

Scout Training Badges and Emblems

The Scout Badge

To be passed under arrangements made by the Scout Leader.

The Arrowhead Badge on a purple background surrounded by a rope in a circle, tied in a reef knot at the bottom.

Requirements

1. Knowledge of the Scout Movement

Show a general knowledge of the Scout Movement and the development of world-wide Scouting.

2. Outdoor Activity

Take part in a Patrol or Troop activity out of doors.

3. Scout Promise and Law

Understand and accept the Scout Promise and the Law.

The Scout Progress Badges

The Scout Standard

To be passed under arrangements made by a Patrol Leader and awarded by the Patrol Leaders' Council.
White symbol with the Arrowhead Badge on a green background with a white border.

Requirements

1. Looking After Yourself:
(a) Pack a rucsac for a weekend camp.
(b) Prepare a personal first aid kit for an expedition.
(c) Light a fire; make a hot drink; cook a simple meal out of doors.
(d) Pitch and strike a hike tent.
(e) Camp out, for at least one night; *or*, in winter, spend at least one night in a hostel or hut as part of a Scout activity.

2. Helping Other People:
(a) Know how to deal with cuts, stings, burns and fainting.
(b) Show ability to direct strangers and have some knowledge of local public transport services and local places of interest or importance, including the location of doctors, police station, fire alarms and public call-boxes.

3. Getting About:
(a) Set a map; know what is meant by a compass bearing.
(b) Show understanding of scale and conventional signs by describing a short route selected on an Ordnance Survey map.

(c) Go on a 10 kilometres (6-mile) hike with a friend of your own age, and on return make a verbal report of a set objective achieved en route (e.g. sketch or obtain specific knowledge about some place or person). This may be carried out at home or abroad.

(d) Demonstrate an understanding of the *Country* and *Highway Codes*.

(e) Find out about a foreign country, work out an interesting route to it, and tell your Patrol about the main things you would expect to find there.

4. Scouting Skills:

(a) Explain how to use and care for a knife and axe. Use a knife to whittle a tent peg (or other object) from a piece of wood, and an axe to prepare wood for a fire.

(b) Demonstrate any three knots, bends or hitches and two lashings useful in camp or on a boat.

(c) Show a general knowledge and interest in weather conditions and signs and, where appropriate, relate these to your home area.

5. Hobbies and Interests:

Demonstrate to your Patrol or Troop some skill or proficiency in a personal hobby or interest. Examples: cycling, swimming, nature study, weather lore, aircraft recognition, stars, horse-riding, model making, basket work, stamp collecting, literature, drawing, decorating, radio construction, joinery. These are examples only, and other interests or pursuits may qualify.

6. Promise and Law:

Discuss with your Patrol Leader your progress in Scouting, including living by the Promise and Law, and plan your future progress.

The Advanced Scout Standard

To be passed under arrangements made by the Scout Leader and awarded by the Patrol Leaders' Council. A triple white symbol with the Arrowhead Badge on a brown background.

Requirements

1. Self-Reliance:

(a) Have camped twelve nights.

(b) Swim 45 metres (50 yards). (Alternatives only permissible at the discretion of the District Commissioner).

(c) Understand the precautions which must be taken, including knowledge of hypothermia (exposure), its causes, prevention, symptoms and immediate treatment, before setting out on any adventurous activity, e.g. sailing, hill walking and caving.

(d) Operate, maintain and be aware of the dangers of misuse of the following:

    (i) modern lamps and stoves;

    (ii) pressure stoves and lamps.

(e) Complete either of the following:

    (i) Know what to look for when choosing a camp site and draw up a complete menu (including quantities) for a two-man weekend camp.

    (ii) Cook a two-course meal for two people in a kitchen or galley.

Service:

(a) Show how to give clear, concise information when calling for an ambulance, the police or fire brigade, and know what action to take in the event of an accident or other emergency including rescue from fire, drowning, electric shock and gas leak.

(b) Know the first aid treatment for external bleeding and shock, the correct method of ap plying respiratory resuscitation, and the dangers involved in moving injured persons.

(c) Carry out some form of voluntary service within or outside Scouting either by doing a worthwhile job of at least three hours duration, or by performing regular service for an equivalent period. This may be carried out at home or while on a visit abroad.

3. Adventure:

(a) Complete *either* a 20 kilometres (12-mile) journey on foot or by water *or* an 80 kilometres (50-mile) cycle journey, camping out overnight with a Scout of your own age. Produce a brief written account of your journey and of what has interested you. This may be carried out in the United Kingdom or as part of a visit abroad.

(b) Use a prismatic or Silva type compass outdoors to complete a simple exercise involving compass bearings.

(c) Explain the contour system and be able to give and locate an Ordnance Survey grid reference.

(d) Complete any two of the following:

(i) Take part with your own Patrol or Troop in a joint outdoor activity with a Patrol from another Troop, either from the United Kingdom or abroad, e.g. camp, hike, wide game or expedition.

(ii) Go alone, or with a friend of your own age: either to a place of interest or on a journey of not less than 40 kilometres (25 miles) using public transport. Give a brief verbal report on the day's events.

(iii) *Either* paddle a single seat canoe for 1500 metres (1 mile) *or* crew a sailing dinghy round a triangular course *or* understand the belay system and abseil properly down 9 metres (30 feet).

(iv) While camping abroad spend a day with your Patrol or with another Scout from your own or a local Troop in exploring a local town or village. On your return, report verbally on what you did, what you saw, whom you met, and what you learnt of local life.

Scoutcraft:

(a) Complete a pioneering project using at least two different lashings and/or blocks and tackle. (This should normally be a Patrol project.)

(b) Demonstrate three knots, bends or hitches useful in rescue, e.g. bowline, triple bowline and recognised belay procedure.

(c) *Either* cook a backwoods meal and eat it *or* make a bivouac and sleep the night in it.

(d) Know the safety rules of axemanship and how to care for a bush saw and felling axe. Use either for felling, trimming or logging up light timber.

(e) Complete any two of the following:

(i) *Either* keep a nature diary about birds and animals over a period of at least one month *or* make a specimen collection of leaves and flowers over a similar period.

(ii) *Either* keep a simple daily weather record for one month *or* maintain the Patrol log for two months.

(iii) *Either* visit an important building or other local feature and compile a short report about it, describing its history and purpose, *or* survey a small area in the vicinity of your home, e.g. half-mile of river or canal, and construct a large scale plan showing its important features.

(iv) Show attainment of a skill or interest by passing a Pursuit Badge.

(v) Demonstrate an awareness of the need for conservation by actively taking part in a conservation project.

(f) Discuss with your Scout Leader:

(i) Your understanding of the Scout Promise and Law.

(ii) Your future Scout training and membership of the Venture Scout Section.

(iii) The practical meaning of the world-wide brotherhood of Scouts.

The Chief Scout's Award

To be passed under arrangements made by the Scout Leader and awarded by the Patrol Leaders' Council. The Arrowhead Badge surrounded by a laurel wreath in gold on a green background.

Requirements

1. Achievement:

Accomplish any *four* of the following skills not otherwise attained in your Scout progress. Not more than two skills may be used from any one group, but at least one skill from three of the groups must be accomplished. You must actually reach the standard required for each skill. Having done so, you may complete your own record by entering in your *Progress Book* the date and place of the achievement, which may be accomplished either alone or with other Scouts, or – whenever possible – in conjunction with Venture Scouts, thereby qualifying you also for part of your Venture Scout Membership Badge. No adventurous activity should be attempted on your own.

(a) **Group A – Challenge**

(i) *Either* paddle a single seat canoe in moving water over at least 3,000 metres (2 miles) *or* sail a dinghy, go about, reach and tack, rig sails and stow properly after use.

(ii) Take part as a member of a properly planned expedition on mountains of 600 metres (2,000 feet) or higher, or negotiate successfully a rock climb on rope, but not as leader (grade: moderately difficult).

(iii) Complete a course of at least 400 metres (¼ mile) on water skis.

(iv) Make a descent on snow skis, in a reasonable style and under control, with not more than two falls, over 60 metres (200 feet) on a slope with a gradient of at least 15 degrees.

(v) Fly a two-seat glider, from take-off to landing, to the satisfaction of an accompanying instructor.

(b) **Group B – Practical**

(i) Change a wheel on a motor vehicle, check and clean sparking plugs, adjust points, check the battery, oil and tyres, and know the greasing points.

(ii) Help to build, maintain and tune a go-kart, and be able to drive it.

(iii) *Either* build a radio receiver – without using a kit (although you may consult circuit diagrams in magazines or books), *or* keep a log of amateur radio broadcasts to which you have listened on a radio receiver over a period of at least three months, including a Scout Jamboree on the Air.

(iv) Have a good practical knowledge of one of the following: care and maintenance of domestic appliances, carpentry and joinery, metal work, home decorating and maintenance.

(v) Take, develop and print three photographs, each being of a different type of subject – e.g. portrait, action shot, landscape, building, shot from an unusual angle.

(c) **Group C – Endeavour**

(i) Make a survival kit of dehydrated and survival foods and live on it exclusively during a 24 hours expedition.

(ii) Make a successful attempt at an outdoor sport or other outdoor interest – e.g. archery, pony-trekking, caving, aqua-sports, fishing tennis, golf. archaeology, geology, conservation.

(iii) Complete:

Either a hike camp, canoe or boat journey of not less than 48 kilometres (30 miles) or cycle tour of not less than 160 kilometres (100 miles), taking at least two days and camping out overnight at a site of your own choice. This may be carried out during a visit abroad. *Or:* a night hike of not less than 16 kilometres (10 miles) between dusk and dawn, over open country, of which at least 3,000 metres (2 miles) must be crossed with the aid of a compass. This may be carried out during a visit abroad.

(iv) Be proficient in the technique of personal survival swimming.

(v) Be proficient in one of the following: gymnastics, judo, fencing, tumbling, trampolining or similar activity.

(d) **Group D – Social**

(i) Help to organise and run *either* a joint training or social activity for both sexes, *or* a hospitality event for Scouts or other visitors from abroad.

(ii) Prepare, cook and serve a full three-course dinner for four people, at a high standard, either indoors or outdoors.

(iii) Camp abroad, or with Scouts from another country.

(iv) Successfully complete some form of residential course other than a Patrol Leaders' Training Course. Your choice is not restricted to courses organised by the Scout Movement.

(v) Take an active part in some form of amateur entertainment, e.g. beat group, amateur theatricals, choral singing and conjuring.

2. Leadership:

(a) Hold the Advanced Scout Standard.

(b) *Either:* complete satisfactorily a course of Patrol Leader training, and guide at least one Scout in your Patrol through the requirements for the Scout Standard; show that all members of your Patrol are making individual progress.

Or: train at least two Scouts to Advanced Scout Standard in two activities, e.g. backwoodsmanship, compass, cooking, emergencies, pioneering.

(c) Show leadership ability in one of the following:

run a Patrol camp at a good standard;

plan and run successfully a Patrol expedition or other activity;

help to plan and run successfully a worthwhile Troop expedition or other activity;

train and lead a team to act as "casualties" for use in first aid training, including the use of make-up for simulations of injuries and symptoms.

3. Responsibility:

(a) Arrange and carry out, either individually or as a member of the Troop, some form of useful service to others either within or outside the Movement, e.g. useful service to handicapped, invalid or infirm person, assistance with some form of public service, such as hospital or welfare home. (A suitable project would require regular voluntary service over a period of at least three months.)

(b) Gain one Service badge and one Pursuit badge since attaining Advanced Scout Standard, or qualification of an equivalent standard from an approved body or society.

(c) Show your acceptance of responsibility at home, or at church, Troop, school or place of work.

(d) Meet personally with the District Commissioner and discuss your present and future commitment within the community and within Scouting.

(Note: This requirement to be taken last).

Scout Proficiency Badges

Scout Proficiency Badges are gained under arrangements as set out in *Rule 9 iii above*.

Interest and Pursuit Badges are on a green background. Service Badges are on a red background. Collective Achievement Badges are on a green background with a red border. Instructor Badges are of the same design as the appropriate Interest, Pursuit and Service Badges and of the same colour background, but have a gold border.

Sea and Air Training Badges are on a dark blue and light blue background respectively; the corresponding Instructor Badges have gold and silver borders respectively.

Advanced Pioneer
(Collective Achievement)

Requirements

1. Pass or have passed the Pioneer Badge.

2. Demonstrate, and know the uses of, the following lashings:

(a) Harvesters hitch.

(b) Double sheetbend.

(c) Fishermans knot.

(d) Rolling hitch.

(e) Figure of eight lashing.

(f) Diagonal lashing.

3. Demonstrate the following:

(a) Sailmakers whipping.

(b) Eye and back splices.

(c) Anchorage for firm and soft ground.

4. Have a knowledge of the following:

(a) The construction of man-made and natural fibre ropes and their breaking strains.

(b) The Aerial Runway Code.

(c) How to store and maintain pioneering equipment.

5. As a member of a group of 3 to 6 Scouts design and build two projects as agreed with the examiner beforehand.

Note: Alternative activities may be undertaken as agreed by the Patrol Leaders' Council.

Advanced Swimmer
(Pursuit)

Requirements

1. Pass or have passed the Swimmer Badge.

2. Demonstrate entry to water by a straddle jump and racing dive.

3. Swim 100 metres in less than four minutes.

4. Swim 800 metres, of which 400 metres shall be on the back, and 400 metres on the front or side (no time limit).

5. Surface dive into 2 metres of water (a) head first, (b) feet first and swim at least 2.5 metres under water on each occasion.

6. Tread water for 3 minutes.

7. Take part in a swimming activity of an advanced nature, e.g. competitive swimming drown proofing, competition diving.

Note: A Scout who has qualified for the Silver Personal Survival Award of the Amateur Swimming Association qualifies automatically for this badge.

Air Researcher
(Pursuit)

Requirements

1. Know the Flight Safety rules as laid down in *Rule II, 72 i & ii.*

2. Carry out a research project over a period of at least three months into one of the following subjects:

Either:

(a) the development of aircraft over one of the following periods:

    (i)   1783 to 1904
    (ii)   1904 to 1918
    (iii) 1918 to 1933
    (iv) 1933 to 1945
    (v)   1945 to 1960
    (vi) 1960 to the present.

Or:

(b) the development of balloons of all types.

Or:

(c) the development of rockets, including man carrying types.

Or:

(d) the development of the jet engine.

In the course of your research, visit at least one place of interest which is directly relevant to your project, e.g. a museum, an air display, a factory.

The presentation of your project must include a model which you have made to illustrate some aspect of your research. Other support material such as sketches, diagrams, slides and cuttings should be used wherever possible.

Air Spotter

(Interest)

Requirements

1. Identify from photographs or silhouettes, shown for ten seconds each, three-quarters of the aircraft in the list published annually by Headquarters for this purpose.

2. Keep a log for three months reporting aircraft seen, giving identities or recognition features, approximate headings, times, dates, etc.

3. *Either:*
(a) Recognise and name national aircraft markings, both service and civil, of at least six contries including the United Kingdom.
Or:
(b) Understand the R.A.F. system of letter designation according to aircraft function and give examples of three such designations.
Or:
(c) Name three basic training aircraft used in private flying. Give a brief report on one, naming a club and airfield where it is used (local wherever possible).
4. Describe the recognition features of six aircraft selected by the examiner.

Ambulance
(Service)

Requirements
Qualify for Essentials of First Aid Certificate of the St. John Ambulance Association, or the Junior Certificate of the St. Andrew's Ambulance Association or the British Red Cross Society.

Angler
(Interest)

Requirements
1. Know the water safety rules. Undertand the dangers of wading and the precautions to be taken.
2. Go fishing in fresh or salt water on at least six occasions in three months. Keep a record of, or discuss with the examiner, these fishing trips showing numbers, species and sizes of fish caught; methods, tackle and bait used; weather and water conditions.

3. Know the dates of the closed seasons and the size limits of salt and/or fresh water fish in the area(s) in which you fish.

4. (a) Be able to identify *either:*

   (i) bass, cod, and mullet; *or*

   (ii) roach, perch, pike, carp, and tench.

(b) Have a knowledge of the habitat and feeding behaviour of the fish identified; know suitable baits and hook sizes.

(c) Know how to handle a fish when landing it.

5. *Either:* Cast with surf tackle a measured 45 metres (50 yards); *or:* cast leger and float tackle into a 1 metre (3ft.) circle at least three times out of six at 9 metres (10 yards) range; *or:* cast a trout size fly line 11 metres (12 yards) with a minimum of splashing.

6. Identify a plug spoon, wet and dry trout flies or nylon paternoster, running leger and bomb and pyramid lead sinkers used in sea fishing.

Archaeologist

(Pursuit)

Requirements

1. Have a knowledge of *one* of the periods of human prehistory (e.g. Paleolithic, Mesolithic, Neolithic, Bronze Age, Iron Age) or of the archaeololgy of Roman Britain.

2. Show an understanding of the importance of the preservation of ancient monuments, the necessity of reporting finds to the nearest museum, and the danger of digging without expert supervision.

3. Have a general knowledge of the methods used by archaeologists for discovering and recognising sites (e.g. field work, aerial photography, etc.) and a knowledge of the process of scheduling ancient monuments, the listing of buildings under the Town and Country Planning Act 1968, and the law of Treasure Trove.

And two of the following:

4. Produce a log with sketches and/or photographs of at least one week's work on a "dig" in which you have assisted.

5. (a) Produce a log of a study made of various periods of church architecture, including sketches made in the field of examples of seven different styles, e.g. Saxon, Norman Transitional, Early English, Decorated, Perpendicular, Renaissance, Gothic Revival and Modern.

(b) Show that parts of a church can be approximately dated by the architectural style.

6. Make a report on objects of two periods (chosen from question 1 and exhibited in a museum).

Note: The report must be illustrated with sketches made in the museum, and show a knowledge of the importance and use of the objects.

7. Visit all the sites possible in an area to be decided upon by the examiner or curator of the local museum; report on the type and condition of each, and draw a sketch map to scale of one of them.

Notes:

(i) The report must be illustrated with a sketch map of the area chosen, with the monuments visited, marked.

(ii) The reporting to a museum of actual or threatened damage to an ancient monument is of great service and should always be done without delay.

8. Carry out an archaeological project chosen by yourself and approved by the examiner, or a museum curator.

Artist
(Interest)

Requirements
1. Paint or draw an illustration of a scene from a story selected by the examiner.
2. Paint or draw a person from life or an object set before you.
3. Paint of draw a landscape set by or known to the examiner.
4. Show the examiner a selection of your recent work.

Astronomer
(Pursuit)

Requirements
1. Recognise the prominent constellations visible throughout the year:-
Winter: Orion, Aries, Auriga, Taurus (Pleiades and Hyades), Canis Major, Canis Minor; and the Circumpolar constellations of Ursa Major and Cassiopeia.
Spring: Leo, Boötes.
Summer: Cygnus, Lyra, Aquila, Delphinus.
Autumn: Pegasus.
2. Recognise and show an elementary knowledge of the following Stars:-
Winter: Sirius, Procyon, Betelgeux, Saiph, Rigel, Aldebaran, Hamal, Capella.
Summer: Deneb, Vega, Altair.
Autumn: Merak, Dubhe.
3. Keep a diary of your observations through the year. This would include sightings of meteor showers, changes of planetary positions, and eclipses.
4. Know the meanings of elementary astronomical terms:- i.e. axial rotation, synodic and

sidereal periods, opposition, conjunction, meridian, ecliptic, celestial equator.

5. Give a general description of the Solar System and the individual Planets, and the Galaxy.

6. Have a good knowledge about landings made or planned on other bodies in the Solar System since 1969, and about man's activities in space.

7. In addition to the observations made in your diary, keep a record of these activities during the year in question, and say how these will contribute towards future space missions.

Athlete
(Interest)

Requirements

Compete in any three events (2 track and 1 field or *vice versa*) and gain points as indicated on the scoring chart.

Minimum points total for award of badge:

Age	Points
Under 12	9
Under 13	10
Under 14	12
Under 15	13
Under 16	14

Notes:

(i) A Scout who has gained the 3 Star Award of the Amateur Athletics Association qualifies automatically for this badge.

(ii) The recommended weights of the shot, discus and cricket ball are 4 kg., 1 kg., and 0.135 kg respectively.

Points	100 Metres Sec.	200 Metres Sec.	400 Metres Sec.	800 Metres Min.	1500 Metres Min.	High Jump Metres	Long Jump Metres	Shot Metres	Discus Metres	Cricket Ball Metres
10	10.7	22.1	49.2	1.52	3.52	1.91	6.90	15.6	51.00	
9	11.2	23.1	51.8	2.02	4.12	1.81	6.30	13.6	42.75	
8	11.7	24.3	55.4	2.12	4.32	1.71	5.67	11.6	35.25	
7	12.6	26.5	59.5	2.22	4.55	1.56	5.00	9.7	28.50	57.00
6	13.6	29.5	64.5	2.36	5.20	1.36	4.50	8.2	23.50	47.00
5	14.6	32.5	69.5	2.56	5.45	1.18	4.00	6.8	19.10	40.00
4	15.6	36.6	74.5	3.16	6.10	1.08	3.50	5.8	16.10	35.00
3	16.6	38.6	84.0	3.36	6.44	0.98	3.16	4.8	13.10	30.00
2	17.6	39.5	94.0	3.56	7.24	0.88	2.83	3.8	9.00	25.00
1	18.6	40.6	108.0	4.16	8.04	0.78	2.50			20.00

Backwoodsman

(Collective Achievement)

Requirements

1. Demonstrate a knowledge of the following:

(a) Exposure and its treatment.

(b) First Aid to Advanced Scout Standard level (*see Advanced Scout Standard, Requirement 2b*).

(c) Construction of different kinds of shelter.

(d) Types of fire and burning qualities of different woods.

(e) Rescue signals involving whistle, torch, Morse, air rescue, ground signals to aid search party.

2. With a group of at least three Scouts take part in a survival exercise lasting approximately 36 hours, during which the group will:

(a) Construct a shelter of natural materials and sleep in it.

(b) Cook all meals over a wood fire. Apart from a knife, cook meals without utensils or aluminium foil.

(c) Make a collection of edible plants and/or fruit.

(d) Demonstrate a suitable method of filtering water and its purification.

(e) Demonstrate methods of direction finding without a compass by day or night.

Notes:

(i) Requirement 1 must be completed before Requirement 2 is undertaken.

(ii) Suitable country for this would be wooded lowlands. Wild mountainous country is not intended.

(iii) Alternative activities may be undertaken as agreed by the Patrol Leaders' Council.

Bellringer

(Pursuit)

Requirements

1. Know the names and functions of various parts of a church bell and its mounting, as hung for ringing changes.

2. Ring with others, i.e. rounds on an 'inside' as well as on a 'leading' bell, and change to a new position in 'call changes' whilst maintaining a good striking performance. Be able to raise and lower a bell unaided.

3. Ring Plain Hunt on the Treble and ring an 'inside bell' to a plain course of at least one 'standard' method other than that used in 4 following.

4. Ring an 'inside' bell for a touch of at least 120 changes of a 'standard' method.

5. Explain, in general terms, how a church bell is made and tuned.

6. Know how to adjust, splice and maintain bell ropes.

7. Write out in full a plain course in a standard method on six or more bells and answer questions thereon.

8. Attend regularly at your own tower for Service ringing and practice for at least three months.

Boatswain

(Pursuit)

Requirements

1. Pass or have passed the Coxswain's Mate Badge.

2. (a) Have a general knowledge of ropes, including different uses, stresses and strains, and demonstrate the correct methods of stowing cables, coiling light lines and painters.

(b) Have a knowledge of sail canvas and terylene, be able to name the parts of a sail and know how to maintain sails in good condition.

(c) Have a good knowledge of both standing and running rigging in:

    (i) one of the Group's open sailing craft;

    (ii) a gaff-rigged vessel;

    (iii) a class racing boat.

(d) Have a practical knowledge of at least three types of purchase tackles.

(e) Demonstrate that you can heave a lifeline 18 metres (20 yards) with reasonable accuracy.

3. (a) Be able to use a palm and needle and make a drogue with canvas.

(b) Make a rope fender for a dinghy.

(c) Make a grommet and stop a block ready for operational use in a sailing boat.

(d) Complete a long splice *or* make up a pair of lizards using bull's eyes or thimbles.

(e) Demonstrate *afloat* in a sailing boat under way the following: single catspaw, running bowline, double sheetbend and mouse a hook.

(f) Pipe 'Away boat's crew'.

4. Take a consistent and practical part in one of the following activities:

(a) constructing a canoe

(b) constructing a hard chine boat

(c) carrying out hull repairs to a carvel, clinker or fibreglass boat

(d) making a spinnaker or stormsail for one of the Group's boats.

5. Take a responsible part in *one* of the following activities:

(a) rig a derrick (or derricks) with rope, spars and tackles, etc., and lift a small dinghy from the water.

(b) rig a form of breeches buoy, using a life-buoy, ropes, tackles and spars, etc., and demonstrate its use.

(c) the launch of a boat from a sandy or shingle foreshore and beaching the craft and hauling up well clear of water. The rigging of a hull strop and the use of a carrick bend to feature in the hauling-up evolution.

6. Taking a leading part in *one* of the following exercises afloat:

Either:

(a) board a sailing boat, apparently dismasted, stream a drogue and ride it, construct and hoist a jury rig, recover the drogue and sail the boat home; the candidate taking the helm. The jury rig to include *one* makeshift mast, two jury sails, a rolling hitch, single catspaw, sheetbend and appropriate lashings. The distance of the operation out and in to be approximately 900 metres (4 cables) each leg.

Notes:

(i) One orthodox sail may be utilised but not in its normal or proper setting.

(ii) In craft carrying two masts, one orthodox mast may be retained to set one jury sail.

(iii) The second jury sail to be fashioned from available materials, e.g. oilskins, canvas covers, sacking, tarpaulins, etc.

Or:

(b) Answer a signal for assistance from a sailing boat with a 'damaged rudder' and 'aground in shallow water' at approximately 900 metres (4 cables) distant. Refloat the craft by warping off, rig for sailing, recover ground tackle and sail the boat home. The candidate to board the 'stranded' craft, supervise laying out of kedge anchor and warping off, recovery of anchor and re-rigging of sailing gear. The candidate to sail the craft home using a steering oar in place of the 'damaged' rudder.

Notes:

(i) The candidate should muster the crew with the appropriate pipe.

(ii) The candidate should supervise preparation of the pulling or power boat with the appropriate gear to include: warp, spare anchor and a drogue.

Camp Cook
(Interest)

Requirements

1. Cook without utensils, but using foil, a two-course meal for yourself and at least one other person.

2. Successfully cook and serve a breakfast such as:

Bacon and eggs;

Scrambled eggs;

Sausages with tomatoes;

Kippers;

Porridge.

3. Successfully cook and serve a meal such as:

A stew with dumplings;

A mixed grill;

Chicken Maryland;

A "main course" dish of your own choice.

4. Successfully cook and serve a sweet such as:

A steamed or boiled pudding;

Stewed fruit and custard;

Fruit fritters;

A sweet of your own choice.

5. Draw up two menus (including quantities) of three courses each (not all of which need require cooking) for a Patrol of six.

Note: All dishes to be cooked under camp conditions and preferably on a wood fire.

Camper
(Pursuit)

Requirements

1. Have camped under canvas with a Troop or Patrol for a total of not less than fifteen nights.

2. Pitch and strike a hike tent.

3. Direct successfully the pitching and the striking and packing of a Patrol tent.

4. Know what to look for when choosing a camp site.

5. Show understanding of the principles of camp hygiene, and the importance of order and cleanliness in camp generally.

6. Demonstrate how to store food in a quartermaster's tent.

7. Construct alone a camp larder, a camp oven and two other gadgets of your own choice.

8. At a camp, cook for yourself and at least one other – but not more than a normal Patrol – *either* a hot breakfast meal, *or* a dish for a main meal which must include two vegetables.

9. Have a good knowledge of *Scout Camping*.

Camp Warden
(Service)

Requirements

1. Have camped on ten separate occasions on at least four different sites.

2. Have worked for at least 7 days at a permanent (District, County or National) camp site, helping the Warden to his satisfaction.

3. Demonstrate three of the following:

(a) Use of charcoal for cooking.

(b) Building a camp fire.

(c) Pitching a Patrol tent.

(d) Drying wet clothes and bedding in camp conditions.

(e) Fire precautions in camp.

4. Explain, and where possible demonstrate, methods used in camp for four of the following:

(a) The care of food.

(b) The care of drinking water.

(c) The care of cooking stoves and of equipment other than personal gear.

(d) The disposal of waste.

(e) The construction and care of latrines.

5. Have a good knowledge of *Scout Camping*.

6. Equip a camp first aid box suitable for a Patrol, for a camp of 7 days duration.

7. Demonstrate the ability to use three of the following:

(a) Felling axe.

(b) Bush saw.

(c) Maul.

(d) Adze.

(e) Pruning tool.

(f) Any mechanical equipment, e.g. grass cutting machine, power-saw, or drill.

8. Discuss with the examiner developments and improvements you would like to see on any permanent camp site with which you are familiar.

Canoeist

(Pursuit)

Requirements

1. Pass, or have passed the Elementary Canoeist Badge.

2. (a) Have a general knowledge of canoe types and equipment.

(b) Demonstrate a simple canoe repair.

(c) Have a knowledge of the British Canoe Union River Advisory Service and the problems of access.

(d) Have a knowledge of safety rules in canoeing.

3. Pack a canoe for a day's expedition and present it for inspection.

4. Demonstrate the following:

(a) Launching, embarking and disembarking.

(b) Paddling forwards and backwards.

(c) Drawing the canoe sideways.

(d) Turning and stopping the canoe.

(e) A suitable support stroke.

5. Demonstrate the following manoeuvres on B.1. waters:

(a) Ferry glide – forward and reverse.

(b) Break in and out of fast current.

6. (a) Perform a capsize drill, and be rescued in deep water.

(b) Perform a deep water rescue of a capsized companion.

7. Swim 45 metres (50 yards) in canoeing clothing.

8. *Either:*

Take part in 3 full day expeditions on B.1. or B.2. waters.

Or take part in 3 competitive canoeing events – slalom, long distance racing, etc.

Or take part in a weekend canoe camping expedition of at least 24 km (15 miles).

Or be a member of a surf rescue team and perform 10 hours service.

Notes:

(i) The examiner must be a member of the British Canoe Union.

(ii) A Scout who holds the 1 Star Award of the British Canoe Union qualifies automatically for Requirement 1 of this badge.

(iii) A Scout who holds the 2 Star Award of the British Canoe Union qualifies automatically for Requirements 1, 4 and 6a of this badge.

(iv) A Scout who holds the 3 Star Award of the British Canoe Union qualifies automatically for Requirements 1, 4, 6a and 6b of this badge.

(v) A Scout who holds the Proficiency Award of the British Canoe Union qualifies automatically for this badge.

Communicator

(Pursuit)

Requirements

To gain the badge you must pass all the requirements in **A** or **B**.

A

1. *Either:*

Send and receive a message of not less than 150 letters at rate 9 (45 letters per minute) in Semaphore, and at rate 5 (25 letters per minute) on buzzer or lamp in Morse.

Or:

Send and receive a message of not less than 150 letters at rate 8 (40 letters per minute) on buzzer and at rate 6 (30 letters per minute) on lamp in Morse.

2. Demonstrate that you know a recognised procedure when sending and receiving a message.

3. Improvise at least two methods of sending a message in Morse or Semaphore at least half a mile at or over rate 4 (20 letters per minute).

4. Know the International Phonetic Alphabet. Give the phonetic names to five groups of five mixed letter groups provided by the Examiner. *Note: 80 per cent accuracy required in all tests. Outdoor sending and receiving stations to be a minimum of 140 metres (150 yards) apart. Buzzer stations to be in separate rooms.*

B

1. (a) Within a period of three months, log 50 different radio amateurs showing details of date, time, call sign, signal strength, readability and location.

(b) Discuss with the examiner your experiences in keeping your log e.g. use of equipment, longest distance covered.

2. Discuss with the examiner the use of the various amateur frequency bands. Know which frequencies you should use to cover various distances during the day and night.

3. Define at least twelve international "Q" signals.

4. Know the Post Office regulations restricting the use of "walkie-talkie" radio equipment.

Note: A Scout who has qualified for the G.P.O. Amateur Radio Licence qualifies automatically for this badge.

Community
(Service)

Requirements

To gain the badge you must pass all the requirements in one of the following alternatives **A, B** or **C.**

A

1. Find out about local community services (e.g. health, education, leisure, social) using such resources as the local authority, youth officer and local library. Discuss with the Patrol Leaders' Council how these services meet the needs of the members of the community.

2. Carry out a study of one aspect of community concern in your area, after consulting the Patrol Leaders' Council and Scout Leader. The study should be of approximately six months duration, and could include the old, the young, the disabled, the lonely or the unemployed.

3. Take a regular part in a form of service to the community, spread over at least two months. Explain to the Patrol Leaders' Council what you have learned from this experience of social involvement.

B

1. Show knowledge of handicaps resulting from impairment of three of the following:

The senses

The intellect

The central nervous system

The heart and lungs
Balance and mobility
Glandular and metabolic functions
Physical development
Normal language attainment

2. Show an awareness of, and describe, four aids to everyday living available to handicapped people.

3. Make a list of statutory agencies and organisations working with the handicapped, including social services, specialist social workers, local 'talking newspaper' group, etc.

4. Have frequent contact with handicapped people for a period of three months.

5. Display a skill relating to one area of handicap e.g.

Deaf and dumb alphabet (finger spelling) or sign language;

Braille;

Wheelchair management and maintenance;

The techniques used in lifting and handling the handicapped.

6. Complete one of the following:

(a) Record a short story or series of poems on tape for the blind.

(b) Make an access survey of public buildings in your town or area.

(c) Accompany a blind person on a shopping expedition or country walk.

7. Carry out one of the following:

(a) Make an aid such as lazy tongs or holding device, book rest, slicing gauge for the blind, non-slip tray mats.

(b) Make a relief map for the blind.

(c) Make a 'route map' recording places of interest that could be followed by a blind person.

(d) Make a training aid for a handicapped Cub Scout, Scout or Venture Scout.

(e) Discuss with your Patrol Leaders' Council and examiner, The Scout Association's policy towards the handicapped.

C

Either:

1. Take part in a visit to a local Police station and find out about:

(a) The organisation of a Police Force and the rank structure.

(b) The various specialist departments.

(c) Communications including personal radio, emergency system and phonetic alphabet.

(d) The practical side of preventing and detecting crime.

2. Show an understanding of crime prevention in the home and the community.

3. Observe a stranger for a period of two minutes and, after a period of time, be able to describe him or her in such a manner as to enable the person to be recognised.

4. Show a good knowledge of the *Highway Code*.

Or

Take part in a locally organised course as agreed by your Patrol Leaders' Council, Scout Leader and the Police Force.

Cook

(Pursuit)

Requirements

1. Know what is meant by normal culinary terms, e.g. au gratin; to bat out; roux; to sweat; fold; render.

2. Prepare successfully two of the following sauces:

Mornay; Apple; Mustard; Parsley;
Hollandaise; Mint.

3. Prepare by yourself and cook two of the following, the choice being your own;

Shepherd's Pie   Plain Omelette

Yorkshire Pudding   Apple Tart
Fruit Cake   Macaroni Cheese.

4. Cook and serve for two to four people two dishes from list (a) and two from list (b);

(a)

Goulash

Beef Olives

Escalope of Veal Holstein

Steak and Kidney Pudding

Boeuf Stroganoff

Casseroled Chicken

With two vegetables cooked so as to conserve their food value.

(b)

Pancakes

Plum Duff

Steamed Fruit Pudding

Buck Rarebit

Apple Dumplings

5. Demonstrate four different ways of cooking potatoes (e.g. baked in jacket, creamed, croquettes, lyonnaise, etc.)

6. Know the principal joints, etc., of pork, lamb, beef, and how to carve a chicken.

Note: At least one of the dishes selected for requirements 3 and 4 to be cooked under camp conditions.

Craftsman

(Interest)

Requirements

The project to be completed for this badge must be agreed with the examiner beforehand, and should last approximately six hours.

1. From your own design, make an object(s) from materials such as wood, metal, clay, plastic, leather or the like. The design should include details of construction.

Cyclist
(Interest)

Requirements

1. Own, or have used satisfactorily for at least six months, a cycle, properly equipped and in good working order.

2. Be able to make simple adjustments and repairs at the discretion of the examiner, e.g. change tyre and tube, mend a puncture, replace a brake shoe and block, adjust the height of saddle and handlebar to enable a younger boy to ride the cycle.

3. Demonstrate that you know and observe the *Highway Code*, traffic signals, lighting-up times, road signs, national system of road numbering and direction, and that you can read a road map.

4. Take part in a Scout activity which includes the use of cycles.

Note: A Scout who has passed the National Cycling Proficiency Test of the Royal Society for the Prevention of Accidents qualifies automatically for those requirements of parts 2 and 3 of this badge covered by the National Cycling Proficiency Test.

Electronics
(Pursuit)

Requirements

1. Demonstrate a knowledge of simple theory of semi conductor devices and how they may be used with components to make useful electronic systems.

2. Demonstrate at least four electronic systems that you have constructed. Show that you are able to modify one to perform a number of different functions. Explain in simple terms the theory of your modifications.

3. List at least four domestic and four industrial uses of electronics, and explain the principles on which one of them works.

Elementary Canoeist

(Interest)

Requirements

Qualify for the British Canoe Union 1 Star Test (Elementary).

Entertainer

(Collective Achievement)

Requirements

Carry out these activities as a member of a group of Scouts, preferably as a Patrol project.

1. Write and plan a short entertainment with your Patrol or group. This could take the form of a sketch, film slide and tape presentation, camp fire or a stage routine involving some of the following: mime, drama, music, story telling, conjuring, photography, sound recording.

2. Prepare your entertainment, ensuring that everyone has a job to do, e.g. actor, producer, stage manager, publicity manager.

3. Present your entertainment at a Pack or Troop Parents' Evening.

4. Discuss with your Scout Leader, or other adult (*see Note ii*) to discuss the value of the work you have undertaken.

Notes:
(i) Alternative activities may be undertaken as agreed by the Patrol Leaders' Council.
(ii) An adult with some expertise in stage entertainment may be consulted to help with the selection of projects and preparation of alternatives.

Explorer
(Pursuit)

Requirements

1. Arrange and carry out an expedition for yourself and at least two other Scouts, preferably members of your Patrol, of not less than two days' and one night's duration, in country not previously visited.

Note: The expedition may be carried out on foot, by cycle, on horseback, by canoe or by boat. All equipment and food for the expedition to be carried by those taking part.

2. Plan a project, and submit it to the examiner for approval; carry it out alone or with a companion, to the examiner's satisfaction. The type of project should be a simple exploration, such as identifying and mapping all footpaths or bridle paths or waterways within a 1.5 kilometres (one-mile) radius of a given point.

3. Complete a journey, with a companion, of 5 kilometres (3 miles) by compass bearings only. Six different bearings by degrees to be used. A map may be used.

Fireman
(Service)

Requirements

1. Understand how your local fire brigade works.

2. Give a simple explanation of the process of combustion, know the effects of smoke and heat, and how to act in smoke. Know the dangers and understand the fire precautions necessary in the home relating to: all types of heating, particularly oil heaters and open solid fuel fires; portable electric fires; airing linen; electric wiring, fuses and appliances, particularly electric blankets; smoking materials, particularly matches; use of household gas, petrol; flammable adhesives; fireworks; candles; bonfires; storage of materials; party decorations; doors and windows.

3. Seek advice from a Fire Prevention Officer or specialist and plan the fire precautions for a Scout, or similar, entertainment, including seating, and know why precautions are necessary.

4. Know the dangers of fire at camp and what precautions should be taken. Know the causes of heath and grass fires and how to deal with an outbreak.

5. Explain what action should be taken, and why, on an outbreak of fire indoors and outdoors. Know the various methods of calling the fire service and the correct procedure to be taken; have knowledge of what happens from the time of the call to its acceptance by the fire service and the reasons for such action.

6. Understand how a bucket chain works. Know how to use a stirrup pump. Know how to use fire extinguishers including water, dry powder, foam and vapourising liquid types and on what kinds of fire they should be used. Know how to deal with a person whose clothes are on fire.

7. Be proficient in making a chair knot and bowline on the bight. Explain the methods of rescue employed; explain and demonstrate crawling with an insensible person.

Forester

(Pursuit)

Requirements

1. Be able to identify in summer and in winter the following trees: Oak, Ash, Sycamore, Beech, Elm, Birch, Horse Chestnut, Lime, Plane, Field Maple, Spruce and Pine. Know how to identify any tree by reference to identification keys, etc.

2. Have a knowledge of the tending of woods and plantations, the sequence of operations and the reason for these operations. Know some of the dangers to which woods may be exposed, i.e. frost, fire and animals.

3. Prepare soil and transplant a young tree.

4. Know how to select and use an axe, how to take care of it and the safety rules of axemanship.

5. Know how to fell and trim out a tree.

Geologist

(Pursuit)

Requirements

1. Show a knowledge of the *Geographical Field Work Code* in the planning of geological excursions.

Note: Copies of this code are available from Scout Headquarters.

2. Go on one (more if possible) geological excursion with a person having local geological knowledge and make a record of what you have seen in a field notebook.

3. With one or more companions, organise a geological excursion. Make observations from a safe vantage point and make a record in a field notebook.

Notes:

(i) Before this trip is undertaken, advice must be sought from, and the route ratified by, a person with sound local geological knowledge.

(ii) On no account must you go on this trip alone. All due safety precautions must be taken.

4. Find out about the geology of the area in which you live.

5. Be prepared to discuss a labelled collection of about 12 geological specimens. (This collection could be your own, from a museum, from school, etc.) The collection should normally consist of the following specimens:

(a) 4 different rock types. Be able to describe how they were formed and their economic use.

(b) 4 minerals. Know their chemical formulas and common names, and where possible, the economic uses to which they could be put.

(c) 4 fossils. Know their names and geological ages, and describe their modes of life.

Guide
(Service)

Requirements

1. Show (wherever reasonable in a practical way) that you know the locality surrounding your home and Headquarters, up to 1.6 kilometres (1 mile) radius in boroughs and urban districts and up to 3.2 kilometres (2 miles) radius in rural districts.

Note: The District Commissioner may, at his discretion, vary the area to exclude undesirable neighbourhoods, parks or other open spaces, and include an equivalent area.

2. Know the location of the following:

(a) Doctors, veterinary surgeons, dentists, hospitals and ambulance.

(b) Fire station, police station, garages, public telephones.

(c) Bus stops, railway station(s), and routes of buses and trains to surrounding areas.

(d) Scout Headquarters, public parks, theatres, cinemas, churches, museums, barracks, public conveniences, and any building or place of local interest.

(e) Homes of your District Commissioner, Scout Leader, Group Scout Leader and the Scouts in your Patrol.

Note: For the Metropolitan Police Area the following alternative to the tests in para. 2 (a), (b), (c) and (d) is permitted at the discretion of the District Commissioner:

Have a sound general knowledge of what parts of the country are served by the main-line railways and how to reach the principal London railway termini, the main motor coach stations, the air terminals, and twelve places of national importance (e.g. The Tower, Zoo, etc.) from your Headquarters or home.

3. Show that you understand how to use a map

of the district and use it to point out at least six examples of 2 above. You should guide the examiner by the quickest route to any place covered by the above.

4. Give directions for a person travelling by public transport or cycle or car to a camp site approximately 8 kilometres (5 miles) away.

Gymnast
(Interest)

Requirements
1. *Either* hold Award 1 of the *Sunday Times* British Amateur Gymnast Association Award Scheme
Or the 3rd Class B.A.G.A. Vaulting and Agility Award.

2. Have a knowledge of how the events in an international competition are organised and the dimensions of the apparatus used.

3. Comment on techniques shown by a junior gymnast performing basic rolls and positions – at the discretion of the examiner.

4. Understand the basic principles of judging.

5. Coach a junior in a basic skill such as a simple vaulting or tumbling movement, a choice given to the candidate by the examiner.

Helmsman
(Pursuit)

Requirements
Qualify for the National Elementary Day Boa Certificate of the Royal Yachting Association.

Hiker

(Collective Achievement)

Requirements

Working as a group of at least three Scouts carry out three hikes as follows:

(i) One of 12–16 km (6–10 miles) day hike.

(ii) Two of 26–32 km (16–20 miles) including an overnight stop, one of which must be in unfamiliar country.

Notes:

(i) Before undertaking each hike the group must provide a detailed route card showing estimated times of arrival; map references; route to be followed; bad weather alternatives; camp sites, etc.

(ii) Each member of the group must also show that he knows the intended route and have a knowledge of simple map reading, the use of a compass, first aid and emergency procedures.

(iii) After each hike the group must provide a verbal report of the expedition. For at least one of the overnight hikes, the group must make a presentation which may be in the form of a tape recording, log book or photographic record.

(iv) Expeditions by canoe, horseback or cycle of similar duration may be acceptable, provided at least one overnight hike on foot is carried out.

(v) Alternative activities may be carried out as agreed by the Patrol Leaders' Council.

Hobbies

(Interest)

Requirements

1. Make a collection or study of objects over a period of at least six months. (The nature or subject of the collection will be chosen by you. Suggestions are as follows: stamps, shells, cheese labels, train spotting and the like.)

2. Discuss with the examiner the reasons for your choice. Know something about the subject of your choice and show an intelligent interest in it.

Horseman
(Interest)

Requirements
1. Have a firm seat independent of the reins and show that you are able to apply simple aids correctly.
2. Have a knowledge of the care and working of a pony or horse off grass.
3. Show that you are able to be in control of a pony or horse on the road and in the countryside. Have a proper regard for road sense, safety and courtesy and for country lore.
Note: A Scout who has qualified for Standard C of The Pony Club qualifies automatically for this badge.

Interpreter
(Service)

Requirements
Pass the following test in any language other than your own:
1. Carry on a simple conversation for approximately 10 minutes.
2. Write a letter of approximately 150 words dealing with a Scout topic.
3. After a few minutes for study, give an approximate translation of a paragraph from a newspaper or periodical.
4. *Either:* Assist as interpreter for a foreign visitor;
Or: Write letters for a Scout Group, school o

similar body, e.g. helping with the arrangements for a foreign visit or exchange;

Or: Correspond regularly and for not less than one year with a Scout or person of Scout age of some other country.

Jobman
(Service)

Requirements

Demonstrate six of the following, the choice to be made by you:

(a) Renew a sash cord, or replace a casement window frame and hang.

(b) Glaze a window, both in wood and iron frames.

(c) Help to paint and paper a room.

(d) Take precautions to prevent frozen pipes in a dwelling house.

(e) Repair defective plastering.

(f) Re-hang a door and repair door furniture, including handles, locks, etc.

(g) Effect minor repairs to furniture, such as broken castors and minor upholstery repairs.

(h) Help to lay a pavement.

(i) Put a neat patch on a garment.

(j) Clean and polish a car.

(k) Repair a gate or fence.

(l) Mix concrete and effect simple repairs with it.

(m) Repair children's toys.

(n) Lay linoleum.

(o) Replace a tap washer.

(p) Oil and adjust a lawn mower.

(q) The immediate steps to be taken in the case of a burst water pipe.

Note: Other options can be chosen by the examiner and you.

Librarian

(Interest)

Requirements

1. *Either:*

Supply the examiner with a list of at least twelve books which you have read in the previous twelve months. Explain why you read them, what you thought of them and answer questions about their contents.

Note: The list should include both fiction and non-fiction, with not more than three books by any one author, and should exclude school text books.

Or:

Supply the examiner with a short bibliography dealing with a subject in which you are specially interested. Explain your choice of books to the examiner and answer questions about their contents.

2. Describe, in simple terms, how a book is made.

3. Show that you know how to use a library catalogue. Explain how fiction and non-fiction books are arranged on the shelves and why they are treated differently.

4. Know what is meant by a Reference Book. What sort of information could you obtain from the following books and how are they arranged?:

Chamber's Encyclopedia
Whitaker's Almanack
ABC Railway Guide
Chamber's 20th Century Dictionary
Who's Who
Bartholomew's Gazetteer of the British Isles
The Guinness Book of Records.

Note: The examiner may substitute a suitable alternative for any title not readily available.

Lifesaver
(Service)

Requirements

1. Hold the Scout Swimmer Badge.

2. Understand and where possible demonstrate the following methods of rescue – the reach, throw, wade and row.

3. (a) Enter the water, swim 50 metres to the subject and tow for 50 metres using a towing aid, e.g. lifebuoy, piece of wood, etc.; land the subject by the stirrup method.

(b) Enter shallow water with a straddle (running) jump, swim 20 metres to a subject considered to be unconscious and not breathing. Tow, using the chin tow to water shallow enough to stand in. Demonstrate mouth-to-nose resuscitation while walking the subject to the side; then secure him in a position of safety.

(c) Jump or dive into the water, surface and swim 10 metres. Recover an object 2.5–4.5 kilogrammes (5 to 10 lbs.) from a depth of at least 1.5 metres (5 feet). Bring to the starting point using life-saving backstroke.

4. Throw an 18 metres (60 feet) lifeline to fall between two pegs twice out of every three throws. Pegs to be 1.2 metres (4 feet) apart and 12 metres (40 feet) from thrower.

5. Show method of rescue in the case of ice-breaking, house fire, gas poisoning, car accident, contact with live electric wire.

6. Using a training manikin where possible, demonstrate the expired air (mouth-to-mouth and mouth-to-nose) method of respiratory resuscitation.

Note: A Scout who has gained the Intermediate Award of the Royal Life Saving Society qualifies automatically for parts 3 and 6 of this badge.

Map Maker

(Pursuit)

Requirements

1. Make a map by triangulation, using prismatic compass or plane table. The area should include fields, a building and a pond or equivalent features.

2. Make a road map, with compass and field book, of two miles of road, showing all main features and objects, within a reasonable distance on either side, to a scale of four inches to one mile. The field book must be produced for inspection.

3. Enlarge such portions of a 1:50 000 scale O.S. map as the examiner may determine, by a 1:3 proportion.

4. Draw a simple cross-section of a 1:50 000 scale O.S. map (line chosen to include varied features, gradients, etc.).

Master-at-Arms

(Pursuit)

Requirements

To gain the badge you must pass all the requirements in one of the following alternatives **A** or **B**:

A

1. Demonstrate proficiency in one of the following: singlestick, quarterstaff, fencing, boxing, judo, wrestling or archery.

2. Have attended regular training sessions in the selected activity for a period of not less than three months.

3. Take part, in the selected activity, in a properly supervised contest and be able to demonstrate the correct methods of attack and defence.

B

1. Know the usual safety-first rules for rifle shooting and have a knowledge of the parts of the rifle you use and of its care and cleaning.

2. Produce two targets fired by yourself, preferably on different dates, within the previous four weeks for any one of the four alternative tests, showing that on both occasions you have obtained not less than the minimum score indicated. The targets must be certified by your Instructors. The edge of the shot hole nearest to centre of the target to decide the value of the hit.

Small Bore Rifle (.22 inch). Any single loading type; any sights except telescopic; position prone: sling may be used. Ten shots at any of the following ranges:

Test	Distance	Minimum Score
1.	23 metres (25 yds.)	80
2.	18 metres (20 yds.)	80
3.	14 metres (15 yds.)	80

For all Tests the Special Proportionate N.S.R.A. Cadet and Schools (1971) Cards should be used.

Air Rifle (.177 inch). Any single loading type; position standing or prone; a sling may be used. Ten shots at the following range:

Test	Distance	Minimum Score	Targets
4.	6 metres (6 yds.)	75	N.S.R.A. 5 Bull Air Rifle (Air 7)

Note: When using air rifles care must be taken to fix the targets so that pellets do not rebound to the danger of the firer's eyes.

Mechanic
(Pursuit)

Requirements

To gain the badge you must pass all the requirements in one of the following alternatives **A, B, C, D** or **E:**

A

1. Know the principles of operation of an internal combustion engine and understand the function of the clutch, gearbox and rear axle differential of a motor car.

2. Remove, clean and check the gap of a sparking plug and show that it is sparking.

3. Clean and set the distributor points. Understand the firing sequence and reconnect all plug leads correctly.

4. Identify the electrical circuits of a motor car protected by each fuse and clean and top up a car battery.

5. Check and top up the level of oil in a motor car engine.

6. Remove and replace a road wheel; know the precautions to observe; check tyre pressures and depth of tread; understand the reasons why cross and radial ply tyres should not be mixed on the same axle.

B

1. Construct a radio receiver using at least two valves or transistors. A temporary layout on a board will be sufficient and headphones may be used, but a construction kit may not be used. Draw the circuit diagram of the set for the examiner and explain to him the function of each main component.

2. Demonstrate ability to use a small soldering iron correctly, and know the particular precautions necessary when using a soldering iron with transistors and printed circuits.

3. Understand the extreme care which is necessary when working with mains operated radio sets, especially the AC/DC type (e.g. when installing an extension loudspeaker or making internal adjustments).

4. Be able to cure a simple fault in a domestic radio set (e.g. faulty switch or lead, noisy controls, high resistance battery).

5. Describe the regulations controlling the issue of licences for TV receivers, radio controlled models and amateur broadcasting.

C

1. Show by demonstration that when operating the engine of power craft you can respond quickly to orders given by the coxswain.

2. *Either:*

(a) Be able to discuss the principles and performances of several types of motor boat engines (other than two-stroke) and show a knowledge of the special care and maintenance needed by a type of small marine internal combustion engine familiar to you (other than two-stroke).

Or:

(b) Have a working knowledge of small motor boat four-stroke engines generally and show a knowledge of the special servicing required by a small marine diesel unit.

Or:

(c) With minimum assistance dismantle, thoroughly service and re-assemble an outboard engine and demonstrate proper fitting to the transom of a boat. Be able to explain how to detect minor faults in starting and running whilst afloat.

3. *Either:*

(a) As driver/mechanic member of a power boat's crew, assist in the preparation of the boat for a voyage by checking the engine for possible minor faults, checking the fuel supply and pump, and mustering the fire-fighting equipment. In response to orders operate the engine whilst getting under way from the quay. Whilst afloat, demonstrate how to deal with minor running defects in compression, ignition, electrics, filters, intake and outlet and in over-oiling. Operate engine to bring craft alongside the quay and shut-down. Lay out a kedge anchor.

(b) Re-man the boat in response to a 'distress call', and under orders, start and operate the engine whilst proceeding to and manoeuvring alongside a 'stranded craft'. This part of the test to include operation of all gears in a confined area of water and a return journey to base, coming alongside with the tide (or current). Know how to leave the engine in a proper manner and how to drain the engine in an emergency.

Or:

(a) Act as mechanic on at least one of the short cruises or expeditions required by condition 3 of the Pilot proficiency badge and be responsible for the *running* of the engine throughout the cruise or journey.

(b) Thoroughly check and service the engine of a motor boat in preparation for the adventure journey required by condition 4 of the Pilot proficiency badge, to include provision of fuel and safe storage, adequate tool kit and effective fire-fighting appliances. Accompany the expedition either as the mechanic or assistant mechanic and be responsible (or jointly responsible) for the operation, care and maintenance of the engine throughout the journey.

D

1. Understand the basic principles of, and be able to point out, the component parts of *either:*

(a) an aircraft piston engine; *or*

(b) an aircraft gas turbine engine.

2. Understand the basic principles of flight of a fixed wing aircraft.

3. Know and be able to demonstrate Aircraft Marshalling signals used by day and night.

4. Demonstrate your ability to carry out four of the following:

(a) Replenish a light aircraft fuel and oil system.

(b) Rig and de-rig a glider.

(c) Piquet a light aircraft.

(d) Change a set of plugs on a light aircraft engine.

(e) Inspect aircraft main and tail (or nose) wheel tyres for serviceability.

(f) Repair a small tear in the fabric surface of a light aircraft or glider.

(g) The pre-use inspection of a parachute and how to put it on and take it off.

(h) Check the control system of a light aircraft or glider for correct sense of movement.

E

1. Know the principles of operation of a two-stroke or four-stroke internal combustion engine and understand the function of the clutch, gearbox, carburettor and transmission of a motor cycle.

2. Remove, clean and check the gap of a sparking plug and show that it is sparking.

3. Clean and set the contact breaker points. Understand the firing sequence of a multi-cylinder engine.

4. Clean and top up a motor cycle battery. Understand the basic electrical circuit of a motor cycle including the frame earth concept. Be able to identify and change a fuse.

5. Check and top up the level of the engine oil.

6. Adjust the tension of the final drive chain.

7. Adjust the front and rear brakes and be able to change a simply connected cable.

8. Describe the procedure for removing and replacing both road wheels.

9. Check the tyre pressure and depth of tread.

Meteorologist
(Pursuit)

Requirements

1. Keep from your own observations a daily record of the weather for at least one month, to include at least four of the following:

Wind force and direction
Cloud type and amount
Weather – using Beaufort
 letters
Temperature
Pressure
Rainfall amount

2. Understand the working principles of the following instruments and construct a simple version of one of them:

Thermometer
Barometer
Sunshine Recorder
Anemometer
Rain Gauge

3. Understand at least three different ways in which clouds are formed.

4. Know the typical weather produced in your own area by 'warm' and 'cold' air masses in summer and winter, noting the different effects of land and sea tracks. Understand the weather associated with a change of air mass at 'fronts.'

5. Know how synoptic weather maps are produced and be able to understand a simple map, with fronts and isobars, similar to those shown on television and printed in some newspapers. Relate your observations, in requirement 1 above, to these maps.

6. Understand the effects of temperature, wind and water on the human body in cases of exposure and exhaustion.

Model Maker
(Pursuit)

Requirements

To gain this badge you must complete all the requirements in one of the alternatives: **A, B, C** or **D.**

A

1. Construct a model aeroplane (use of kit permitted) which, when flown, meets one of the following minimum flight performances:

Glider (hand launched) – 25 seconds

Glider (tow launched with 50 metres (164 feet) maximum line length) – 45 seconds

Rubber-powered – 30 seconds

Engine-powered (15 seconds maximum motor run) – 45 seconds

Control line: Demonstrate your model by making a smooth take-off, three laps level flight at approximately 2 metres (6 ft) and climb and dive with a smooth landing.

2. Have a knowledge of the basic principles of flight, including the three axes and their effect on stability and control.

B

1. Build an electric or engine-powered model boat or yacht, not less than 45 cm (18 in) in length (kits permitted) and show it to be capable of maintaining a straight course of not less than 23 metres (25 yards).

2. Give a clear explanation of Archimedes' Principle.

C

1. *Either:*

Build an electric slot car racer (not from a kit, though commercial body and other parts may be used) and drive it to a minimum distance of 122 metres (400 ft) on any track without stopping or leaving the slot more than four times.

Or:

Build a free running car of any type (kits permitted) and demonstrate that it will run for at least 18 metres (20 yards). Airscrew drive allowed.

2. Know how track and wheelbase are measured and sketch and explain Ackerman steering.

D

1. Build a coach or wagon and demonstrate that it runs satisfactorily behind a locomotive.

2. Build a scenic model such as a station, farmhouse, etc. (kits allowed) to scale for a layout.

3. Draw an electric circuit for a simple track layout.

4. Detail the safety precautions to be taken when assembling such a layout.

Note: The Association's Headquarters will provide, on request, conditions for the badge for a Scout whose needs are not dealt with in the above requirements.

Mountaineer

(Pursuit)

Requirements

To gain the badge you must complete all the requirements in one of the following alternatives **A**, **B** or **C**:

A

1. Demonstrate that you have a knowledge of a mountain area covering at least 52 square kilometres (25 square miles), by producing journey notes and log books of journeys in the area. These notes must show:

(a) That you are personally acquainted with the principal routes to summits and the approximate time it would take to complete various day journeys in the area.

(b) That you are acquainted with places of interest in the area, such as: nature conservancy, water conservancy, quarrying or mining, and have some knowledge of them.

(c) That you know: nearest telephones, doctors, inns and places of refreshment and shelter in the area.

(d) That you know the map references and telephone numbers of all rescue posts in the area.

2. Plan a route card for a day journey in the area from a 1:50 000 scale Ordnance Survey map, work out map references (6 figure), bearings and time required from one point to another on journey; also show escape routes and alternatives should you be overtaken by adverse weather. Show that you know of local dangers, the exact location of crags and how best to avoid them.

3. Using a map, demonstrate your ability out of doors to identify open mountainous country; all features seen on land should be identified on map and vice versa.

4. Discuss local weather conditions and demonstrate your ability to understand weather forecasts such as appear in the daily press and on television.

5. Show a knowledge of your equipment:

(a) What you would wear.

(b) What you would carry in a day rucsac.

6. Outline in detail the procedure in event of an accident:

(a) Care and treatment of patient, what can best be done by person remaining with an injured person.

(b) Exact information a rescue post wishes to have.

(c) How and with what to give a distress signal.

(d) Procedure for an emergency bivouac.

7. Demonstrate your knowledge of exposure:

(a) Causes of exposure and exhaustion.

(b) How to avoid exposure and exhaustion.

(c) Recognise symptons in a person suffering from exposure and exhaustion.

(d) How to deal with a person suffering from exposure and exhaustion (on a mountain and at base).

8. Have a knowledge of the contents of the publication *Safety on Montains* (Sports Council).

B

1. Show your knowledge of ropes used in rock climbing:

(a) British Standard Specification and breaking strains and lengths.

(b) Care of a climbing rope, including coiling storage and recognition of a damaged section and when a rope should be discarded.

2. Demonstrate your ability to tie yourself to:

(a) The end (bowline and two half-hitches).

(b) The middle (figure 8 knot).

3. Demonstrate your ability to select, test and make the following:

(a) Spike belay, using main rope.

(b) Thread belay, using suitable sling and karabiner.

(c) A running belay.

4. Show your understanding of the calls used in rock climbing.

5. Demonstrate your ability to abseil down a rock face (not less than 5 metres (15 feet)) with a safety rope.

6. Take part in at least five rock climbs of a standard not less than "moderately difficult", such climbs to be led by an experienced climber, who will judge and report on your competence.

7. Have a knowledge of the contents of the publication *Safety on Mountains* (Sports Council).

C

The requirements set out out in Book 1 of the *Mountain Craft Checklist and Logbook* available from Headquarters.

Musician
(Interest)

Requirements

To gain the badge you must complete all the requirements in one of the following alternatives **A, B, C, D, E, F, G** and **H**.

A

1. Sing a solo with chorus or take part as treble, or alto, in a part song.

2. Read at sight three tunes.

3. Know what is meant by a sonata, concerto and oratorio, and give three examples of each.

4. Discuss with the examiner recent performances you have heard at concerts or on radio or television.

B

1. Play two solos, one of your own choice and the other at sight, on any recognised musical instrument other than a percussion instrument.

2. *Either* produce a concerted item with others, in which you must play the instrument used in (1) above, *or* play another solo of different type and speed than those played in (1) above.

Note: A certificate that you are a regular member of an orchestra may be accepted.

3. Know what is meant by a sonata, concerto and oratorio, and give three examples of each.

4. Discuss with the examiner recent performances you have heard at concerts, or on radio or television.

C

1. *Either:*

(a) Sing unaccompanied two different types of folk song – e.g. spiritual and sea shanty, mountain song and lullaby.

Note: You may add your own rhythm, such as hand-clapping or tambourine.

Or:

(b) Sing, with your own accompaniment (banjo, guitar, mandolin, etc.), two different types

113

of folk song.

(c) Play two different types of folk song as music on a banjo, guitar, mandolin, concertina, harmonica or other folk song instrument.

2. Know some basic principles and fundamentals of music, such as tuning your own instrument, keys, chords and bass notes.

Note: Folk music is at its best when simple and uncomplicated. The Scout should be encouraged to put over his knowledge in his own way.

3. Discuss with the examiner some of the types of folk music and performers or artists which you enjoy. You must be prepared to give reasons for your choice.

D

1. Show that you can tune your pipes properly.

2. Play two bagpipe marches in 2/4 time.

3. Play two bagpipe marches in 6/8 time.

4. Play a slow march or slow air.

5. Play a march, strathspey and reel. (The march may be one of those played in (2) above).

Note:

(i) *All tunes to be of your own choice.*

(ii) *When Northumbrian or Irish pipes are used, alternatives may be used at the Examiner's discretion.*

E

As a Percussion Drummer:

1. Be a member of a musical group, either at school, in your Scout Group, or other organisation.

2. Take part in a stage presentation.

3. Perform routine maintenance on your instrument.

4. Perform basic drum rudiments.

5. Play a good class roll in the following form:

    3 paces roll;
    5 paces roll;
    7 paces roll.

6. Take part satisfactorily in six different pieces of music.

F

1. Be a member of a Band in which you have served for the minimum of six months, either at school, in your Scout Group or other organisation; and provide proof of regular attendance.

2. If a member of a uniformed, marching Band:

(a) Present yourself for examination in full and correct Bandsman's uniform and demonstrate an understanding of why a Bandsman's turnout should be smart and correct.

(b) Demonstrate your proficiency in basic drill movements including marking time, turns, wheels, counter-marching and carrying of instruments; in both quick time and slow time.

3. Present your instrument and accessories for inspection and demonstrate your ability to perform routine maintenance and, where applicable, tuning of your instrument.

4. Take part satisfactorily in six different marches, playing one of the undermentioned instruments:

SIDE DRUM

(a) Beat in 2/4 and 6/8 time.

(b) Play "off" beats in 2/4, 6/8 and 3/4 time.

(c) Play a good class roll in the following form:

    (i) 3 pace roll;

    (ii) 5 pace roll;

    (iii) 7 pace roll.

(d) Show a good stick drill when playing at the halt and on the march.

TENOR DRUM

(a) Beat in 2/4 and 6/8 time.

(b) Play "off" beats in 2/4, 6/8 and 3/4 time.

(c) Play a good class roll in the following form:

    (i) 3 pace roll;

    (ii) 5 pace roll;

    (iii) 7 pace roll.

(d) Show good stick drill when beating at the halt and on the march.

(e) March over a distance, not less than 50 metres, beating a strict 116 paces to the minute.

(f) March over a distance, not less than 50 metres, beating in slow time – 65 paces to the minute.

BASS DRUM

(a) Show good stick drill when beating at the halt and on the march.

(b) March over a distance, not less than 50 metres, beating a strict 116 paces to the minute.

(c) March over a distance of not less than 50 metres, beating in slow time – 65 paces to the minute.

BUGLE OR TRUMPET

(a) Demonstrate an understanding of the terms 'attack' and 'tone'.

(b) Perform 'tongue' and 'slurred' notes.

(c) Play as a solo three of the following:

'Sunset' or 'Retreat';

'Last Post' or 'Second Watch';

'Reveille';

'General Salute'; *or*

'Cookhouse'.

FLUTE OR FIFE

(a) In respect of the six marches (4 above) these marches should be:

    (i)   At least two marches in 2/4 time.

    (ii) At least two marches in 6/8 time.

    (iii) A slow march or slow air.

    N.B. These marches are to be played whilst actually marching along and, if necessary, may be accompanied by other flutes or fifes to complete harmonics.

(b) Play two solo pieces of your own choice.

BELL LYRES

Play two solos of your own choice.

CYMBALS

(a) Show good cymbal drill when playing at the halt and on the march with simple 'flourishing'.

(b) March over a distance, not less than 50

metres, beating a strict 116 paces to the minute.

(c) March over a distance of not less than 50 metres, beating in slow time – 65 paces to the minute.

DRUM MAJOR

4 above does not apply.

(a) Explain your understanding of a Drum Major's control of his Band, and the importance of:

    (i)   Clear signals and words of command.

    (ii) The ability to make–on–the–spot decisions.

(b) Command your Band to fall in correctly and dress off.

(c) Control your Band while playing (at the halt) a march; a fanfare or salute; and 'Retreat' or 'Sunset'.

(d) Demonstrate, whilst on the march with the Band, signals for 'right wheel', 'left wheel', 'countermarch', 'mark time', 'short step', 'advance', 'open-order march', 'close-order march', 'stop playing', 'recommence playing' and 'halt'.

(e) Demonstrate your ability to march correctly in quick time and slow time, whilst carrying the stave.

(f) Demonstrate the correct method of returning a salute when carrying the stave, both at the halt and on the march.

(g) Demonstrate simple showmanship with the stave, both at the halt and on the march.

(h) Explain the corrective measures you would adopt when faced with the following three possible emergencies that could arise during an otherwise routine parade or display:

    (i)   Animals.

    (ii) Traffic.

    (iii) Other bands.

G

1. Be a regular member of a handbell team, either at school, in your Scout Group, or other organisation.

2. Take part in a stage presentation.

3. Know how to care for a set of handbells.

4. Be able to read music appropriate for hand-bell ringing, and translate this through a good striking technique.

H

1. Know the names and functions of various parts of a handbell.

2. Be capable of ringing any two handbells in both 'rounds' and 'call changes', maintaining a good striking performance.

3. Ring the trebles for a plain hunt to a max-imum of 8 bells.

4. *Either*

Ring the trebles for a touch of 120 with no. 2 as an inside bell working in a standard method.

Or:

Ring the tenors for a touch of 120 of a standard method with the leading tenor, (i.e. 5 or 7) working as an inside bell.

Or:

Ring two inside bells for a plain course in a standard method of more than 5 bells – minor, triples or major.

5. Explain in general terms how a handbell is made and tuned.

6. Write out plain courses of a least two stan-dard methods or show a knowledge of these methods.

Naturalist
(Pursuit)

Requirements

1. Study the natural history (i.e. plant and animals) during any two of the seasons (i.e. Spring, Summer, Autumn and Winter) of *either*:

    (a) a piece of woodland★

or (b) a piece of parkland★

or (c) a piece of downland★

or (d) a piece of moorland★

or (e) a piece of sea shore, sand-dune or rocks★

★*approximately one acre (5,000 square metres or half Hectare) in size*

or (f) a length of hedgerow†

or (g) a length of roadside verge†

or (h) a length of stream, river or canal†

or (i) a small pond.

†*not less than 90 metres (100 yards)*

Explain the results of the study to the examiner, using field notes, simple sketches or photographs and sketch maps.

2. Discuss with the examiner how the natural history of the site studied could be affected by man's activities or management; e.g. replacing deciduous trees with conifers; waste oil discharged by oil tankers at sea; cutting hedges and roadside verges by machine instead of manually.

3. Make a detailed study of any one plant or animal (i.e. ferns, grasses, wild flowers, trees and shrubs; butterflies, moths or other insects; amphibians, wild animals, birds, fish, etc.)

Discuss with the examiner the results of observations and sources of any information used, i.e. museums, books, etc.

Navigator
(Pursuit)

Requirements

To gain the badge you must pass all the requirements in one of the following alternatives **A**, **B** or **C**.

A

1. Using examples set by the examiner, show that you understand the purpose of the following features of a 1:50 000 scale and 2½-inch Ordnance Survey map; scale; National Grid Reference; True, Grid and Magnetic North; contour lines, and conventional signs.

2. Have a good knowledge of the traffic signs and signals as illustrated in the *Highway Code*.

3. Prepare an A.A. or R.A.C. type strip-route map for use by a motorist or motor-cyclist for a journey of 80 kilometres (50 miles) set by the examiner.

4. Accompany a motorist as a passenger and act as navigator for a journey of 160 kilometres (100 miles).

Notes:

(i) Roads other than A class roads should be used for at least half the journey, and motorways may not be used for more than a total of 32 kilometres (20 miles).

(ii) At the discretion of the examiner this journey may be made by motor-cycle or other alternative forms of transport.

5. Take part in a properly organised orienteering event, competitive or otherwise.

B

1. Given a series of three headings and corresponding tracks, work out in each case the type and the amount in drift in degrees and illustrate each case by a simple diagram.

2. Demonstrate with a compass how an aircraft can be turned on to three successive compass headings.

3. *Either:*

Draw on a topographical air map a track for an imaginary flight of not less than 80 kilometres (50 miles) and point out the landmarks which would show up on both sides of the track in clear visibility at an altitude of about 600 metres (2,000 feet).

Or:

Identify on a topographical air map landmarks seen during a flight of about half an hour's duration in clear weather.

4. Illustrate by means of a simple diagram how a fix can be obtained from two position lines; describe briefly two ways in which bearings can be obtained in an aircraft, thus enabling position lines to be drawn on a chart.

5. (a) Given the true heading and the variation and deviation, work out the compass heading on which the pilot should be flying.

(b) Given two sets of true, magnetic and compass headings, work out the variation and deviation in each case.

6. Illustrate by simple diagrams latitude and longitude.

7. Draw on a topographical map the track between any two places not less than 100 kilometres (60 miles) apart and measure the exact distance; given the aircraft's air speed as 130 km/h (80 mph), work out the time of flight from overhead starting point to overhead destination in each of the following conditions:

(a) With no wind at all;

(b) With a head wind of 30 km/h (20 mph).

(c) With a tail wind of 50 km/h (30 mph).

C

1. Have a good working knowledge of charts, including the projection, datum and symbols used and the tidal information given.

2. (a) Read a mariner's compass marked in points and degrees and have a knowledge of compasses generally, including variation and deviation.

(b) Be able to apply variation and deviation to a compass course or bearing to obtain a true reading; given a true reading to obtain a compass course.

(c) Understand how compass error can be found from a transit bearing.

3. (a) Understand the theory of how a position may be found from any two position lines.

(b) Plot a position from any three cross bearings. Understand what is meant by a 'cocked hat' and how to use it safely.

(c) Plot a position using the 'running fix' method.

(d) Plot a position using a combination of compass bearings and any one or more of the following:

Radio direction beacons
Vertical sextant angle
Horizontal sextant angle
Line of soundings
Transits.

4. Have a working knowledge of tide tables and tidal stream atlases.

5. Understand the use of the marine log to obtain distance run and speed.

6. Understand the buoyage system for United Kingdom coastal waters and other methods of marking dangers and channels.

7. Undertake a coastal voyage of at least 6 hours acting as navigator. A log must be kept showing the courses steered, distance run navigation marks passed and weather experienced.

During the voyage:

(a) Plot the estimated position every hour by keeping up the dead reckoning.

(b) Whenever appropriate, and not less than once per hour, plot an observed position by bearings or other means of obtaining a fix.

The voyage, which need not have a definite destination, should be planned on the chart beforehand using tidal streams to the best advantage and giving hourly courses to steer for an assumed speed.

Observer

(Interest)

Requirements

1. In Kim's Game, remember 24 out of 30 well-assorted articles after one minute's observation. Test to be performed twice running with different articles and each article to be adequately described.

2. By hearing alone, recognise 8 out of 10 simple sounds.

3. Give an accurate report of an incident lasting not less than one minute and involving three persons. This report, oral or written, must include a full description of one of the persons involved, selected by the examiner.

4. Make six plaster casts of the tracks of birds, animals, car or cycle. All casts to be taken unaided and correctly labelled with date and place of making. Two at least to be of wild birds or animals.

5. Follow a trail of one mile length containing approximately 40 signs made of natural materials. The route to be over unfamiliar ground. Roads may be crossed but not followed.

Parascending
(Pursuit)

Requirements

1. Have a knowledge of the Rules in *P.O.R.* relating to Access to Airfields. Understand the factors involved in selecting the launch point on the field.

2. Successfully complete the British Association of Parascending Clubs' Parascending Ground Training, including landing rolls and inflation and collapse of canopy by wing-tip holders and parascenders.

3. Carry out the British Association of Parascending Clubs' Course of Training in controlled descents, and self-released flights up to the standard of 360 degree stable turns.

4. Carry out canopy control practice on the ground and have a basic knowledge of the flight and steering principles of the canopy.

5. Understand and perform the duties of wing-tip holder, look-out and tensiometer reader, and understand the function of the launch marshal.

6. Understand the care, packing and storage of equipment.

Note: A Scout must not attempt the requirements of this badge until he has reached his fourteenth birthday.

Photographer
(Interest)

Requirements

1. *Either*

Produce twelve photographs taken by yourself These must include a minimum of six black and white prints processed and printed by yourself

Or:

Produce a pin-hole camera.

2. Discuss with the examiner:

(a) The main features of a camera (i.e. shutter speeds, apertures, depth of focus, film speed and lens focusing) and how they are used to ensure technically good results.

(b) The various types of camera currently available.

(c) The use of accessories such as tripods, exposure meters, filters and close-up lenses.

3. Describe the processes involved in developing and contact printing a black and white film. Mention briefly the process involved in producing enlarged prints.

4. Diagnose faults in exposure and processing (e.g. camera shake, depth of field, under/over exposure, blurred image).

5. Demonstrate a knowledge of photographs by artificial light by arranging equipment provided by yourself or the examiner for a portrait, still life or similar subject.

Pilot
(Service)

Requirements

1. *Either:*

(a) Pass or have passed parts 1, 2, 3, and 4 of the Boatman Badge.

Or:

Possess the National Elementary Day Boat Certificate of the Royal Yachting Association.

(b) Take charge of a boat and carry out basic manoeuvres. The term 'boat' may include pulling boat, sailing dinghy or canoe.

2. (a) Read a mariner's compass marked in points and degrees and have a knowledge of compasses generally, including variation and deviation.

(b) Be able to read a chart and understand the abbreviations and signs used; explain the use of the compass; the meaning of the term 'Chart Datum' and be able to apply the precipitation of tides to the chart.

(c) Know the different types of buoys, beacons, lighthouses and light vessels in general use, the usual danger, storm, fog and distress signals, including distress signals from aircraft.

(d) Understand the use of the barometer in forecasting the weather and be able to discuss the Beaufort wind and sea scales.

(e) Have a detailed knowledge of the steering and sailing rules, including lights, sound signals and certain visual signals.

(f) Have a thorough knowledge of local boating rules, including harbour regulations, river authority regulations, water restrictions and local rescue and lifesaving services.

3. *Either:*

(a) Complete a series of not less than three cruises or short expeditions afloat in local waters. The cruises to relate to a study of local waters in connection with pilotage and weather conditions. All cruises to have certain objectives and must be organised to include the following:

(i) Ability to lay off three courses on the chart, making due allowances for tidal streams, etc. The courses planned need not have a definite destination but must be varied to cover an area specified by the County Water Activities Committee which shall normally be at least 15 nautical miles coastwise by 3 nautical miles seaward, or as similarly adapted for the larger estuaries. Undertake the three journeys in relation to the projected courses, plotting positions at regular intervals using the three methods of cross bearings, transits and dead reckoning.

(ii) One cruise under cover of darkness

(under supervision if considered desirable, compatible with local sea conditions) to familiarise candidate with navigation lights, lighted channels, moving and anchored sea traffic, beacons and other relevant features.

(iii) To demonstrate that the candidate has a good knowledge of the tides, directions and strength, rise and fall and able to take soundings with lead and line and sounding pole in deep and shallow water respectively.

(iv) To observe sea traffic on the move, including fishing craft riding to their gear and be able to specify recognised fishing and any rights associated with the grounds.

(v) To have a knowledge of local hazards such as unusual weather conditions, sandbanks and bars, rocks and fouled ground, underwater obstructions such as unmarked wrecks, groynes, stakes and any other dangerous features peculiar to the area, and be able to identify buoys, beacons and other marks of caution, including sound warnings.

(vi) To be able to advise on suitable moorings and anchorages, for different types of craft and emergency landing places for small craft.

(vii) To be able to transmit and read the letter 'U' when made by lamp or on siren in Morse.

Or:

(b) Complete at least two cruises, one up river and the other down, to the extent of approximately 48 kilometres (ideally this will mean 24 kilometres each journey but this may be varied (e.g. 32 plus 16) according to local circumstances), by *either* pulling boat, motor boat, sailing boat *or* as leader of two double-seater canoes or three single-seater canoes in company. Both cruises to have certain objectives and must be followed by the completion of a detailed report, in the form of a log but preferably in the form of notes, supported by diagrams and sketch maps. The objectives to include actual sightings and observations related to the following:

(i) Tidal information (approximate heights of tide at Springs and Neaps), periods of ebb, slack water and flood respectively. Pole soundings at regular intervals, with particular reference to channels and entrances to lesser waterways en route.

(ii) Limits of navigation for different types of craft, speed restriction, bridge clearances, lifting procedures (where applicable).

(iii) Buoyage systems, beacons, withys and other warning marks (underwater power cables, etc.); shallows, obstructions, outfalls, and other dangerous features such as weirs on non-tidal waters.

(iv) Information about currents on non-tidal waterways, the effect of heavy rain upriver, danger levels, rapids, and wild water, locks (attended and unattended), lock working, winches, rollers, portages, lock fees and anticipated time delays.

(v) River or Waterway Authorities involved, licences and registration fees, general regulations.

(vi) A good knowledge of the private banks, fishing rights and private waters, riparian owners and landing stages only available by permission.

(vii) Public moorings, hire moorings, boatyards and facilities, i.e. crane availability, slipway and wetdock facilities, ship chandlery and launching sites, with particular reference to car-top and trailed craft.

(viii) Car parking facilities at popular mooring and landing sites, petrol stations and garages adjacent to the riverside, telephones post offices and at least one hospital in the area.

(ix) Camp sites suitable for youth organisations and other sites including fresh water supplies, general food supplies.

(x) Towns and villages with historic interest, railway stations and main road links.

(xi) Commercial waterway traffic, wharves and some knowledge of cargo embarked or disembarked.

Note: The Scout should normally be in charge of the boat in which these cruises are undertaken and much of the information may be compiled in advance, but if local conditions are difficult, i.e. tidal waterways with heavy commercial traffic, etc., an adult observer may accompany the crew to advise in certain circumstances.

4. Accompany the crew of a pulling, sailing or motor boat undertaking an adventure journey, either as a member of the crew or additional to complement, and act as pilot for the journey.

Notes:

(i) The journey may be that specified under the 'Adventure' section of the Coxswain's Mate badge, but the candidate may not count this same journey towards qualification for that badge.

(ii) The candidate may be in charge of the crew.

(iii) The candidate can act as pilot to the crew from another youth organisation undertaking a similar journey provided all the conditions can be met.

(iv) The journey may be that also specified under the 'Expedition' section of the Coxswain Badge and if the candidate is in charge of the expedition, subject to successful achievement he may count this same journey towards qualification of both Coxswain and Pilot badges.

(v) The journey to be of at least twenty-four hours duration and to include a night spent in camp. The outward distance to be of six miles or more.

(vi) The alternative condition (as approved in relation to local conditions) under the 'Expedition' section of the Coxswain badge may also count towards the award of the Pilot badge, provided the candidate

leads (and pilots) the expedition and at least three single-seater canoes take part. All other conditions with regard to the pre-journey summary and after discussion and verbal report must be accomplished.

(vii) The Scout will be expected to submit in advance a brief summary (in note form with diagrams) of the course and destination, tidal or current data, anticipated moorings, times involved and emergency communications.

(viii) On return the candidate will be expected to be able to discuss the expedition in relation to the journey, indicating fairly accurately on chart the actual course pursued with the aid of cross bearings and transits, etc., taken during the voyage. Special attention should be given to states of tides and/or currents, depth of water at entrances to harbours, channels and smaller rivers, etc., and verbal report of any peculiar sightings which may include lights, weather condition, water traffic, etc.

Pioneer

(Collective Achievement)

Requirements

1. Demonstrate and know the uses of the following knots and lashings: sheetbend; clove hitch; round turn and two half hitches; bowline; timber hitch; sheepshank; square and sheer lashings.

2. Demonstrate the following:

(a) West Country or simple whipping.

(b) The correct way to coil a rope.

(c) The use of simple blocks and tackle.

(d) The use of levers to extract or move heavy weights.

(e) An understanding of the need for supervision and safety in pioneering projects.

3. As a member of a group of 3 to 6 Scouts, complete the following:

(a) Take part in an indoor pioneering project.

(b) Take part in building a pioneering model.

(c) Take part in constructing an outdoor pioneering project.

Note: Alternative activities may be undertaken as agreed by the Patrol Leaders' Council.

Power Coxswain

(Pursuit)

Requirements

1. Pass or have passed parts 1, 2, 3 and 4 of the Boatman badge.

2. Have a detailed knowledge of the steering and sailing rules for power and sailing vessels and show by demonstration, using diagrams or models, that you have a practical knowledge of local waters, including:

(a) Tides (or currents);

(b) Local hazards, sandbars, shallows, rocks,

under-water obstructions and any dangerous features such as weirs;

(c) Lights, daymarks and buoyage in relation to local water traffic, including fishing craft and fishing grounds;

(d) Alteration of course and turning signals.

3. Know the safety precautions necessary in power craft, including the proper use of fire-fighting appliances and 'man overboard' drill.

4. Have a knowledge of the elementary principles of the motor boat engine and *by demonstration afloat* show:

(a) That you can start the engine, operate the gears and understand the effect of transverse thrust with a single screw.

(b) That you can turn circles using reverse gear, control the boat in confined waters and stop the engine when going slow ahead.

(c) That you can operate the correct towing procedure, including disposition of crew, and that you are familiar with the use of the kedge anchor in an emergency.

(d) That you can recognise the minor faults in an engine in relation to compression, ignition, battery and charging system, fuel supply and filters, intake and exhaust outlet.

5. Take charge of a small crew and prepare the boat for service, to include the provision of all equipment. Supervise checking the engine, fuel and pump, and then:

(a) With minimum assistance, cast off *with the tide (or current)* ahead using the spring method. Steer a compass course (as set by the examiner) and anchor correctly. With the assistance of a second craft with anchor, demonstrate the use of the kedge anchor. Recover the ground tackle, get under way and return alongside *against the tide (or current) without using reverse gear.* Moor with spring and headrope.

(b) In response to a 'distress' signal, take charge of the crew, cast off *with the tide (or current) astern,* using the spring and headrope method and proceed to a 'stranded craft' (aground in confined waters). Approach across the tide (or current) and take aboard a 'survivor'; manoeuvre clear, using reverse gear, and proceed to pick up a 'body' (not an actual person) from the water. Bring your boat alongside *with tide (or current)*, using reverse gear, giving appropriate orders to crew, and make fast. Supervise preparations necessary to disembark the 'casualty'.

Notes:

(i) The above conditions are designed for the use of inboard power craft and this type of craft should be used if practicable.

(ii) For the use of outboard motor craft the tests should be modified accordingly, e.g.:

4. (a) include some "additional practical knowledge in care and maintenance of outboard engine" and "mixture of fuel and lubricant".

4. (b) delete reverse gear requirement.

4. (d) modify accordingly.

5. (b) delete use of reverse gear entirely and substitute "veer down on wreck using anchor" and when returning alongside (with tide) substitute "using a drogue".

Quartermaster

(Service)

Requirements

To gain the badge you must complete all the requirements in alternative **A** or **B**.

A

1. Have assisted the Group or Troop Quartermaster effectively for a period of six months.

2. Understand and be prepared to demonstrate:

(a) The care of ropes, i.e. whipping, splicing, hanking, coiling, inspection and storing.

(b) The care of tentage, i.e. guyline repairing,

simple tear repairing, reproofing, inspection and storing.

(c) The care of tools, i.e. sharpening, re-setting, re-hafting, cleaning, inspection and storing.

(d) The care of cooking equipment, i.e. repairing, cleaning, inspection and storing.

3. Understand and demonstrate how to keep simple and efficient records, including issue and returns of Group or Troop equipment.

4. Understand and be prepared:–

(a) To demonstrate storage of Cub Scout equipment.

(b) To demonstrate storage of Cub Scout handcraft material.

(c) To illustrate a simple colour, number or other code system for the replenishing of Cub Scout handcraft material.

5. Understand the care and storage of Group visual aid equipment, e.g. projector, wall charts, drawing materials, drawing paper and special visual aids.

6. Understand how to deal practically with depreciation of all equipment.

7. Understand that general tidiness is the secret of good quartermastering. Explain how this is achieved in your own Troop or Group.

B

1. Have assisted the Camp Quartermaster at a Troop Camp or Pack Holiday of at least five days duration.

2. Understand and be prepared to demonstrate the care of all equipment in camp:

(a) Ropes, i.e. coiling and hanking, inspection and storing.

(b) Tentage, i.e. emergency guyline repairing, emergency tear repairing, inspection.

(c) Tools, sharpening and cleaning, inspection and storing.

(d) Cooking equipment, i.e. cleaning, inspection and storing.

3. Understand and demonstrate how to keep simple, efficient records in camp, including issue and returns of all equipment.

4. Understand and be prepared to demonstrate how to care for all other special equipment in camp, e.g. uniforms, hiking kit, climbing kit and canoes.

5. Produce a set of menus covering 48 hours in camp. Be prepared to discuss them with the examiner.

6. Describe how you would deal with storage of food in camp.

7. Submit to the examiner a list of tools you would take to camp, to effect emergency repairs of all equipment. Justify your inclusion of each item in the list.

8. Understand that general tidiness is the secret of good quartermastering. Explain how this was achieved in the camp at which you helped the quartermaster.

Race Helmsman
(Pursuit)

Requirements

1. *Either:*

(a) Pass or have passed parts 1, 2, 3 and 4 of the Boatman Badge;

(b) Have a knowledge of the steering and sailing rules, local rules, distress, storm, fog and danger signals.

Or:

Possess the National Elementary Day Boat Certificate of the Royal Yachting Association.

2. Have a good working knowledge of the yacht racing rules of the International Yacht Racing Union and have a knowledge of the Portsmouth Yardstick Handicapping System.

3. Show by demonstration afloat that you are a proficient helmsman. The demonstration to include:

(a) Sailing the boat in any direction on all points of sailing: tack, wear, reach, run and reef. The boat to be manned by helmsman and one crew.

(b) Two race starts by a five-minute gun with:

    (i)   wind aft on the first leg;

    (ii) wind due ahead on the first leg.

(c) Three turns at a mark:

    (i)   When close-hauled, leaving mark to windward;

    (ii) when close-hauled, leaving mark to leeward;

    (iii) when wind due aft.

(d) Hoisting of a spinnaker when running for (c) (iii).

4. Demonstrate afloat:

(a) "Man overboard" drill when 'on the wind' and when 'off the wind'.

(b) Capsize drill.

Note: If the stress and strain on gear is likely to be

severe if the exercise is repeated, the candidate should observe a controlled capsize.

5. Have some knowledge of modern standing and running rigging, sails and equipment and be able to recognise at least three different classes of modern racing craft.

6. Be able to discuss elementary tactics in relation to racing under sail with particular reference to:

(a) 'searoom';
(b) 'establishing an overlap';
(c) 'giving way';
(d) 'calling for water';
(e) the use of the drop-keel generally;
(f) spinnakers and balloon jibs;

and show that you understand the general organisation associated with events, including preparatory signals, starting signals, recall signals and special signals.

7. Give a reasonable performance as helmsman in a series of three races against boys of your own age. Each race to be between at least three boats and the course in each event to be triangular and over a distance of approximately 2.5 kilometres (1½ miles).

Note: The candidate will be judged on general performance rather than on the results of the races. The races may be specially staged or be part of the programme of a Scout Regatta.

Secretary
(Service)

Requirements
To gain the badge you must pass all the requirements in one of the following alternatives **A, B** or **C:**

A

1. *Either:*
Write with a good legible hand, 250 words prose.

Or:

Type 100 words, with not more than five mistakes, and show how to clean the machine and replace the ribbon.

2. Show an understanding of committee procedure including preparing an agenda and taking minutes.

3. Know how a personal bank account operates and how to write a cheque.

4. Write a letter on a subject chosen by the examiner.

5. Draft a wording for an invitation card addressed to members of the public in connection with a Group, Troop or Patrol event.

6. Show a general knowledge of postal rates in the United Kingdom and know where to find information on parcel post, registered post, recorded delivery and foreign letters services.

7. Prepare a press release on a Group event or write an article for a Scout magazine reporting a Troop, Group or District event.

8. Know how certain items of office machinery operate, such as duplicators and photocopiers.

9. Explain what is meant by 'budgetary control'.

10. Carry out the duties of secretary of your Patrol, the Patrol Leaders' Council or some other committee not necessarily concerned with Scouting, for a period of three months.

B

1. Show a general knowledge of the administrative arrangements of a Scout Group.

2. Show an understanding of committee procedure including the preparing of an agenda and taking minutes.

3. Have a general knowledge of the financial structure of a Scout Group.

4. Know how a personal bank account operates, and how to write a cheque.

5. Explain what is meant by 'budgetary control'.

6. Write a letter on a subject chosen by the examiner.

7. Prepare a report to show awareness of the need for safety precautions.

8. Explain the principles of insurance and have an elementary knowledge of two kinds of insurance.

9. Prepare a press release on a Group event or write an article reporting a Troop, Group or District event.

10. Administer a Patrol for a period of three months.

11. Give a short talk to the Troop demonstrating your knowledge of 1 to 9 above.

C

1. Have a general knowledge of the financial structure of a Scout Group.

2. Know how to write up a cash book.

3. Know how a personal bank account operates, and how to write a cheque.

4. Maintain a Patrol subscription book for at least three months, seeing that the balance agrees with the actual cash in hand.

5. Understand what is meant by delivery notes, invoices, statements of account and be able to check them.

6. Know how to prepare receipts for money received.

7. Explain what is meant by 'budgetary control' with particular emphasis on fund raising.

8. Prepare a simple receipt and payment account for a Troop or a Patrol and report on it to the Troop or Patrol Leaders' Council.

Skier
(Pursuit)

Requirements
1. Demonstrate the following:
(a) Climbing, side stepping.

(b) Straight schuss descent.

(c) Snowplough glide descent to a controlled stop.

(d) Diagonal traverse to left and right.

(e) Four linked consecutive right and left snowplough or basic swing turns.

2. Carry out the following:

(a) Direct controlled side-slip of at least 5 metres (15 feet) in either direction.

(b) Diagonal controlled side-slip of at least 5 metres (15 feet) in either direction.

(c) Four to six consecutive basic swing or parallel turns.

(d) Non-stop no falls descent through at least six open gates.

(e) Swing to the slope to a stop from a steep traverse.

3. Answer five questions from the One Star and five questions from the Two Star British Junior Alpine Ski Test Education questions, available from the National Ski Federation of Great Britain, 118 Eaton Square, London, S.W.1.

Notes:

(i) Ski-ing may be done on snow or artificial slopes.

(ii) Holders of the British Junior Alpine Ski Test One Star Test are excused Part 1 of this badge.

(iii) Holders of the B.J.A.S.T. Two Star Test qualify for this badge automatically.

(iv) Holders of the S.C.G.B. 3rd Class running test are excused Parts 1 and 2 of this badge.

(v) Holders of Nordic or Alpine Ski Awards may well qualify for part, or all, of Parts 1 and 2 of this badge.

Skin Diver
(Pursuit)

Requirements
1. Swimming test. (All tests in this group to be taken without equipment):

(a) Swim 200 metres free style (front only).

(b) Swim 100 metres using any back stroke.

(c) Swim 50 metres wearing a weight belt. The weight should vary according to age and build (at 11 years of age 2.5 kg should be sufficient. Weight may be increased by 0.5 kg per year up to a maximum of 4.5 kg).

(d) Float on back for 5 minutes. (Hand and leg movements permitted.)

(e) Tread water with hands above head for 1 minute.

(f) Recover a brick or similar object from 2 metres depth 6 times in succession.

(g) Show a knowledge of the following:
- (i) Dangers of anoxia.
- (ii) Dangers of eardrum rupture.
- (iii) Pressure equalisation of 'clear ears'.

2. Snorkelling test (using fins, mask and snorkel):

(a) Fit equipment in pool, sinking it in 2 metres of water and diving for each item in turn.

(b) Fin 200 metres.

(c) Perform 3 forward and 3 backward rolls.

(d) Hold breath for 30 seconds under water.

(e) Fin 15 metres under water with snorkel removed.

(f) Fin 50 metres wearing a weight belt (as in Requirement 1(c)) place mask and belt on bottom of deep end of pool. Fin 50 metres using snorkel with face submerged. Retrieve weight belt and mask, fit on, then fin a further 50 metres. (This test must be performed without taking a rest or support).

3. Lifesaving test:

Tow another person 50 metres by a method which incorporates expired air resuscitation giving two or three breaths in the water. Land patient and continue resuscitation at pool side.
Notes:
(i) The examiner must be a qualified member of the British Sub-Aqua Club.
(ii) A Scout who holds the Snorkeller Award of the British Sub-Aqua Club qualifies automatically for this badge.

Smallholder
(Interest)

Requirements

To gain the badge you must complete all the requirements in one of the following alternatives **A, B,** or **C:**

A

1. Have a good knowledge of the farming practices of your locality, with a more detailed knowledge of those of the parish in which you live.

2. Know the farm organisation and daily and seasonal operations of the farm *either* on which you live *or* one of your own choice, with special reference to the livestock, crops, cultivations and machinery and labour force of the farm.

3. (a) Discuss with the examiner and give an account of the changes in the farm practices that have taken place recently in the parish, with particular reference to the starting or giving up of crops or types of stock, and the reasons for these changes.

(b) Produce a set of 12 photographs, of at least eight different seasonal jobs that cover a whole year, taken by yourself on the farm of your choice, and give a brief description of what they represent (simple snapshots are sufficient).

142

B

1. Cultivate out of doors an area of at least 17 sq. metres (20 sq. yds.), for a year, during which time three kinds of hardy annual flower, three kinds of vegetable and two kinds each of bulbs, herbaceous plants and flowering shrubs or roses shall be grown successfully. (As an alternative, eight types of vegetable may be grown instead.)

2. Discuss with the examiner the work you have done in your garden and the results achieved.

Note: The examiner should visit the garden at least four times during the year.

C

1. Keep any kind of livestock for a year

(a) If the animal is a small animal (dog, cat, rabbit, mouse, tortoise, etc.), know its breeding habits, and how the animal should be fed, housed, exercised and trained.

(b) If the animal is a farm animal (e.g. horse, cow, sheep, pig or goat), know how it should be fed and housed, its breeding habits and economic use. Show you know how to handle the animal (e.g. ride horse, milk cow).

(c) If the 'animal' is a bird:

   (i) cage bird – keep, feed and care for the bird.

   (ii) domestic bird (hen, bantam or pigeon) – keep, feed and care for the bird. Know the uses of the bird and how to handle it.

(d) If the 'animals' are bees, keep and manage a hive of bees for a year; know their uses and show some of the produce.

(e) If the 'animals' are fish:

   (i) Set up and keep an aquarium containing a proper balance of fresh water fish and plant life. (A minimum stock of three fish is to be kept.)

   (ii) Discuss with the examiner the keeping of the aquarium during the year, with particular reference to the results obtained.

Notes:

(i) The examiner should be appointed at the start of the twelve-month period.

(ii) Headquarters will provide, on request, conditions for this badge for a Scout whose needs are not dealt with in the above requirements.

Speleologist
(Pursuit)

Requirements

Note: It is essential that an experienced and competent speleologist be in charge of all practice for this badge and whenever any practical aspect of it is undertaken.

1. Thoroughly explore a pothole which requires at least 12 metres (40 feet) of rope ladder or wire ladder and which is at least 120 metres (400 feet) long. You must take a major part in the belaying and positioning of at least 12 metres (40 feet) of the ladders and the subsequent removal of them.

2. Thoroughly explore a cave of minimum length 150 metres (500 feet) which involves a tight crawl of at least 8 metres (25 feet) and one other difficulty such as a traverse of 3 metres (10 feet) or more; a rope pitch of 5 metres (15 feet) or more, a window exit, several changes of level.

3. Know the safety rules for caving and potholing and know the reasons for them.

4. Know the minimum standards for equipment and know how to maintain it.

5. Demonstrate how to lifeline. Whilst doing so, be able to arrest a weight (equal to your own) which is attached to the free end of the lifeline and which has been allowed a free fall of 1.5 metres (5 feet).

6. Do two of the following:

(a) Make a sketch map with accurate dimensions of a cave at least 120 metres (400 feet) long which is not straight.

(b) Take photographs underground of six different features of caves and their formations and correctly label them.

(c) Know the geological reasons for the formation of caves and potholes and their formations and colourings.

Sportsman
(Pursuit)

Requirements

1. Have a good knowledge and know the rules or laws of two outdoor or indoor games such as Rugby Football, Association Football, cricket, tennis, volleyball, table tennis, badminton. Be capable of acting as an official, such as referee, linesman or umpire, in a game organised for young people (school, youth club, Troop or Pack).

2. Take an active part in one winter and one summer team game and show reasonable proficiency and evidence of a sportsmanlike approach to the games.

3. Be able to discuss with the examiner the advantages which can be gained from participation in sport and show that you have a good knowledge of the history of two games chosen by yourself.

4. Know the names and performances of two international, national or local sportsmen. Be able to discuss these personalities with the examiner and show that you have made a study, or have carried out some research, concerning the sportsmen of your choice.

Note: The Association's Headquarters will provide on request, conditions for this badge for a Scout whose needs are not dealt with in the above requirements.

Swimmer

(Interest)

Requirements

Perform the following:

1. Swim 200 metres by any stroke.

2. Swim two of the following (other than the stroke used in Requirement 1):

(a) 50 metres front crawl;

(b) 50 metres back crawl;

(c) 50 metres breast stroke;

(d) 50 metres butterfly stroke.

3. A standing dive from the side of the bath.

4. Demonstrate a shallow water entry, swim 25 metres in light clothing, tread water for one minute, and undress in the water.

5. Understand and explain how you would effect a rescue using the following methods; reach, throw, wade and row.

6. Surface dive in two metres of water and recover, with both hands, an object from the bottom. Return to the side of the bath holding the object with both hands.

World Conservation

(Collective Achievement)

Requirements

Carry out these activities as a member of a group of Scouts, preferably as a Patrol project. Carry out one activity from each of the following sections:

Skill

1. (a) Create a scented garden for a blind person;

(b) Adopt a pond and carry out conservation work and maintenance, obtaining permission and expert advice as necessary;

(c) Build a hide, use it for observing wildlife (preferably staying overnight) and report your findings;

(d) Assist with the preservation of a stretch of water, e.g. stream or canal;

(e) Survey a derelict site, recording how nature has started to reclaim it. Plan and, where possible, take action to further reclamation.

Knowledge

2. (a) Explain the dangers to health of cigarette smoking, or alcohol or drugs;

(b) Explain how different types of pollution in soil affect growing plants. Describe the safeguards that need to be taken;

(c) Explain the pollution caused by the motor vehicle. Describe how this affects people, plants and buildings and, where possible, illustrate your findings;

(d) Explain the causes of water pollution and what action could be taken to lessen the effects;

(e) Explain how governments, industries, and other agencies are helping people to become aware of conservation;

(f) Explain how trees are useful to man.

Understanding

3. (a) Prepare a check list of do's and don'ts for campers and hikers, so that natural things are neither destroyed nor harmed. Give a copy of the list to each member of the Troop;

(b) Find out all you can about animals, birds, plants or fish which are in danger of extinction in your own country. Find out what can be done to save them and, if possible, help to do so with expert advice;

(c) Explain why so many animals in the world are threatened by extinction and suggest what your Patrol can do to assist in their survival;

(d) Make a list of ways in which the Troop camp could contribute to pollution, suggest ways of preventing this and arrange for them to be discussed by the Patrol Leaders' Council before your next camp;

(e) Plan and carry out a conservation project with members of a Venture Scout Unit.

Telling Others

4. (a) Plan a campaign to conserve energy

    (i) At home

    or

    (ii) At school or work

    or

    (iii) At camp

    or

    (iv) At Troop meetings.

Support your campaign with posters, displays, information for the press, and advertising material;

(b) Help to make a nature trail for a Cub Scout Pack;

(c) Help a Cub Scout Pack to build bird tables or nesting boxes;

(d) As part of the plans for an expedition, devise a project to improve the environment. Carry out the project and report on it at a Parents' Open Evening, or a similar occasion;

(e) *Either:*

Survey your local area to find examples of how man has damaged nature. Show how this can be avoided. Send the results of your survey to the appropriate authorities.

Or:

Survey your local area to find examples of how man has tried to improve his environment. Send a letter of appreciation to the appropriate bodies.

Notes:

(i) Alternative activities may be undertaken as agreed by the Patrol Leaders' Council.

(ii) An adult with some expertise in conservation may be consulted to help with the selection of projects and preparation of alternatives.

World Friendship
(Interest)

Requirements

1. Have corresponded regularly (i.e. about once a month) for not less than six months with a Scout of a Commonwealth or other country either individually or as part of a Patrol or Troop "link-up".

2. Carry out a study of a country of your own choice and discuss with the examiner the differences in the way of life between that country and your own.

3. *Either:*

(a) Keep an album or scrapbook for at least six months giving illustrated information (gained from correspondence under 1 above) on Scout activities, sports, home life and national affairs of the other's country.

Or:

(b) Submit a set of not less than 20 photographs or colour slides taken by yourself illustrating and explaining Scouting, life, people, customs and scenery of another country.

4. Complete any two of the following:

(a) Camp or hike for at least seven days with a Scout or Scouts of another country (either in your own or their country) and produce a log book covering this event to include your impressions and knowledge gained of the visiting Scouts and their country or countries.

(b) Entertain in your home for not less than three days a Scout or Scouts from overseas.

(c) Tell the examiner ways in which you have welcomed immigrant young people or visitors from another country met at school, sport or in your local community and what you have done to make them feel at home there.

(d) Give separate, informative talks to your Troop and to a Cub Scout Pack (each of at least

5 minutes duration) on the interest and knowledge gained from your international experiences.

(e) Make a tape recording of camp fire songs from another country or a simple conversation with a Scout in another language, with the meaning of each sentence in English.

(f) Devise and run a Troop or Patrol activity based on information gained from an overseas Scout with whom you are in touch or from your own knowledge of another country or countries.

Instructor Badges

Instructor Badges are available for all Scout Proficiency Badges and are gained under arrangements made by the examiner appointed by the District Executive Committee. No more than two Instructor Badges may be held.

Requirements

1. Hold the proficiency badge in the subject.

2. Have a knowledge of the proficiency badge requirements sufficient to enable you to instruct a Scout in that subject.

3. Attend a training course covering the technical skills involved and the use of training methods.

Note: A leaflet setting out a recommended programme of such a course may be obtained from Headquarters.

4. Assist with the training of Scouts in the subject over a period of at least three months.

Note: This requirement will be taken last.

★The gaining of certain external instructor awards, e.g. St. John Ambulance, Royal Life Saving Society, National Cycling Proficiency Scheme, automatically qualify a Scout for the appropriate Instructor Badge. Details of these exemptions can be obtained from Headquarters.

Sea Training Badges

Boatman

Requirements

Preparation

1. Swim 50 metres in clothes, and thereafter remain afloat for five minutes.

2. Know the safety rules that apply to boating, and appreciate the effect of wind, tide and currents.

3. Name the parts of a boat and its equipment and understand the maintenance of the boat.

4. Have some knowledge of rescue by boat.

Practice

5. Demonstrate, whilst afloat, the following and their correct uses: reef knot, sheet bend, double sheet bend, round turn and two half hitches, fisherman's bend, bowline; make a sailmaker's whipping.

6. Heave a lifeline from a boat.

7. Prepare an anchor, row a dinghy single-handed and anchor.

8. Scull a dinghy over the stern to pick up an object from the water.

9. Pull in a boat's crew, be able to steer a boat.

Project

10. Take part in a half-day's exercise afloat to show that you have prepared yourself for boating; have pursued the basic skills of boatwork, and be able to carry out a simple rescue operation by boat.

Note: During the Boatman training, it is intended that the opportunity should be taken to undertake some canoeing and some sailing as a member of a crew.

Coxswain's Mate

Requirements

1. Possess the Scout Standard.

Approach

2. Possess the Boatman badge.

3. Have a knowledge of the steering and sailing rules; local rules; distress, storm, fog and danger signals.

4. Understand capsize drill and resuscitation of the apparently drowned.

5. Know how to obtain weather forecasts and understand their importance.

6. Hoist the correct colours for a Sea Scout Troop and make "The Still" and "Carry On" on a Bosun's call.

7. Demonstrate how to take soundings in local waters.

Activities

8. Take part in cleaning and painting a boat and assist with repairs to a boat; make an eye splice and short splice.

9. Demonstrate, whilst afloat, the following and their correct uses: clove hitch, rolling hitch and a form of stopper knot.

10. Act as a Coxswain of a boat's crew; carry out basic manoeuvres including anchoring and taking a small boat in tow.

11. Rig a sailing boat and point out and name parts of the gear.

12. *Either:*

(i) Hold the Elementary Day Boat Certificate of the Royal Yachting Association.

Or:

(ii) Show that you are an efficient member of a sailing crew and take the helm and sail the boat on all points of sailing including getting under way and coming alongside.

13. Act as Coxswain's Mate in a rescue exercise, board the "stranded" craft and bring it ashore single-handed.

Adventure

14. Form part of a crew of a pulling boat for an expedition of not less than 24 hours duration, to include a night spent in camp.

Notes:

(i) It is intended that during the Coxswain's Mate training, opportunity should be taken to obtain some experience in the management of outboard or inboard power craft. Alternatively, a short canoeing expedition in company with other canoeists should be undertaken.

(ii) A basic knowledge of chartwork should be introduced during this stage, including some compass work afloat.

Coxswain

Requirements

1. Possess the Advanced Scout Standard.

Exercise

2. Possess the Coxswain's Mate badge.

3. Read a chart and plot a position.

4. Have a good knowledge of the buoyage system; aids to local pilotage; navigation lights; sound signals; tides.

5. Discuss the Beaufort Wind and Sea Scales and know at least two natural signs for fine weather and characteristic signs for approaching bad weather in your local area.

6. Know the skills of personal survival for emergencies in the water.

Efficiency

7. Undertake a repair to a boat using relevant materials.

8. Make a rope fender, a boat's bag out of canvas or a decorative piece of ropework e.g. a lanyard.

9. Send a message of 25 letters over a distance of approximately 330 metres (1½ cables) between two boats or between boat and shore. Be able to recognise the importance of single letter hoists of the International Code of Signals (1969).

10. Take charge of a boat with crew in response to a distress call, take the boat away, steer a short compass course and pick up a small object from the water.

11. Take charge of a party preparing a boat for sailing, including gear to ensure the safety of the craft and crew under all conditions.

12. *Either:*

(i) Hold the Intermediate Day Boat Certificate of the Royal Yachting Association.

Or:

(ii) Be able to sail the boat in any direction on all points of sailing, and be able to tack, wear, reef, make and shorten sail and be able to get under way and come alongside from any direction, anchor safely, and be able to sail up and make fast to a buoy.

13. Whilst afloat, make up a form of sea anchor from available materials in the boat, hove to and understand its use in an emergency.

14. Under sail demonstrate "man overboard" drill using a lifebuoy or similar procedure.

Expedition

15. *Either:*

Take charge of an expedition of 24 hours minimum duration approximately 10 nautical miles distance, under sail or power, to include a night in camp, or sleeping aboard. Some aim or purpose should be attached to the expedition, with evidence of adequate planning in advance (or suitable alternative, according to local conditions and practicability).

Or:

Make a full report of a journey carried out by canoe or small craft, of not less than 32 kilometres (20 miles). The report to include full details of two camp sites adjacent to mooring places in the area.

Notes:

(i) During Coxswain Badge training, every opportunity should be taken to gain experience in charge of power craft, with knowledge of fire-fighting methods and precautions afloat. Instruction should be given in the handling and use of flares. Elementary navigation should be included at this stage, and where opportunity affords, some offshore cruising in larger craft should be arranged.

(ii) Scouts who gain the Coxswain Badge are permitted to wear it on Venture Scout or Venture Sea Scout uniform to show that they hold specialist qualifications.

(iii) A Venture Scout is permitted to qualify for and wear the Coxswain Badge, provided he has satisfied the requirements of the Boatman and Coxswain's Mate Badges either by gaining these badges as a Scout or by meeting the necessary requirements (excepting Requirement 1 of the Coxswain's Mate Badge and Requirements 1 and 2 of the Coxswain Badge).

Air Training Badges

Airman

Requirements

Flight Safety and Airmanship

1. Have a knowledge of the Rules in *P.O.R.* relating to Access to Airfields.

Aviation Knowledge

2. Know the parts of an aircraft, the control surfaces, and how they work.

3. Identify, either from pictures or in flight, 12 aircraft in common use today:

    4 civil commercial aircraft;

    4 military aircraft;

    4 light private aircraft.

Practical

4. Using a model 'chuck' glider, trim it to perform the following manoeuvres:

    straight glide;

    glide with a turn to the left and right;

    stall and dive.

5. Build and fly one of the following:

    A model glider.

    A rubber-powered model aircraft.

    A kite.

    A hot air balloon.

Senior Airman

Requirements

1. Possess the Scout Standard.

Flight Safety and Airmanship

2. Possess the Airman badge.

3. Have a knowledge of the Rules in *P.O.R.* relating to flying.

4. Know how a parachute works, how to put it

on and demonstrate the correct landing procedure.

Or:

Know how the simple life-saving jacket works and be able to demonstrate its use fully clothed in at least 2 metres (6 feet) of water.

Aviation Knowledge

5. Know and be able to demonstrate aircraft marshalling signals used by both day and night. Know the signals in use on an airfield, including those on the signals square, lamp and pyrotechnic.

6. Assist the pilot of a light aircraft in moving his aircraft, strapping in, starting up, taxi-ing, parking and unstrapping and refuelling.

Or:

Assist a glider pilot with ground handling and launching his aircraft and be able to assist him after a field landing.

7. Know the reason for cloud formation and the type of flying conditions to be expected in each basic type. Know how wind speed is measured and know the weather limitations imposed on various air activities.

8. Know the conventional signs in use on the air map and be able to point out the features overflown on an imaginary cross-country route of at least 50 nautical miles flying at a height of 600 metres (2,000 feet). Understand the working and the errors of an aircraft type compass.

9. Pass one of the following:

(a) *Aircraft Recognition.* Be able to identify from photographs or silhouettes shown for 10 seconds, 75 per cent of the aircraft published in a list annually by Headquarters.

(b) *Airline Operation.* Know at least six airlines by name and describe six routes operated by each, together with the aircraft used on each route. Plan a journey to a destination in the Antipodes giving airline, aircraft, date/time of departure (local time), en route stops and date time (local) of arrival, including flying and elapsed times.

(c) *Aerospace.* Understand the reason for weightlessness in orbit or trajectory and the thrust obtained by rockets. Demonstrate a knowledge of a particular current space programme and its purpose.

(d) *Military Aviation.* Understand the R.A.F. system of letter designation according to aircraft duties. Know and be able to describe the military aircraft operating from the U.K.

(e) *Private Aviation.* Name the basic types of training aircraft in use in civil aviation. Give a brief description of one type. Name one airfield and club operating this type.

Practical

10. Build and fly a free flight model aircraft of built-up construction of at least 60 cm (24 in) wing span.

Or:

Build and demonstrate a control line model aircraft to the satisfaction of the examiner.

Or:

Build a non-flying model aircraft with working control surfaces operated by a control column.

11. Have had an air experience flight in an aircraft other than as a fare-paying passenger.

Master Airman

Requirements

1. Possess the Advanced Scout Standard.

Flight Safety and Airmanship

2. Possess the Senior Airman badge.

3. Know the basic rules of airmanship for light aircraft flying and gliding.

4. Understand the system of controlled air spaces. Know the phonetic alphabet.

Aviation Knowledge

5. Understand the basic principles of flight of both a fixed and rotary-winged aircraft.

6. Understand the basic principles of both the piston and jet engine, and be able to point out the component parts of each. Be able to use the tools associated with the servicing of a light aircraft engine, and be able to assist in simple routine servicing.

7. Know the weather associated with frontal system in the U.K. and be able to interpret the Synoptic Chart, indicating the type of weather expected at various points. Know the dangers of thunderstorms, icing and fog on light aircraft.

8. Know how to prepare an air chart for a navigational cross-country flight of not less than 50 nautical miles. Know the basic method of plotting, pin-pointing, determining a heading, given a track and windspeed and direction. Where possible, demonstrate this in the air.

9. Complete one of the following. (This need not be the same subject as that passed for the Senior Airman badge):

(a) *Aircraft Recognition.* Be able to identify from photographs or silhouettes, shown for 10 seconds, 80 per cent of the aircraft published annually by Headquarters. Know the main international markings.

(b) *Airline Operation.* Carry out a project on any airline, giving a brief history, information of the fleet, route structure and the number of passengers carried in the previous year.

(c) *Aerospace.* Show that the scale of the Solar System is understood by preparing a drawing or model of the relative positions of the planets and their main satellites. Understand the stages of acceleration and separation for a satellite to go into orbit round the earth and the re-entry problems. Have a knowledge of the fuel system used in space rockets and for the control of a satellite.

(d) *Military Aviation.* Build from photographs a solid model of a foreign military aircraft

Discuss the various significant features of the design and how they will affect its performance in its designated role.

(e) *Private Aviation.* Know the procedure for inter-airfield flights: filing flight plans, including

    (i)   alternative airfields;
    (ii) safety equipment to be carried;
    (iii) minimum safety altitudes;
    (iv) obtaining weather forecasts;
    (v) knowing weather limitations for visual flight;
    (vi) crossing an airway;
    (vii) papers to be carried;
    (viii)customs requirements.

Practical

10. *Powered Flying.* Have had sufficient qualified dual instruction to be able to take off, fly round the circuit and position the aircraft for a landing.

Or:

Gliding. Have had sufficient qualified dual instruction to fly a glider from take-off to landing, planning your own circuit.

Or:

Research. Undertake some form of advanced project over a period of three months and build a demonstration model to explain the results.

Notes:

(i) Scouts who gain the Master Airman badge are permitted to wear this badge on the Venture Scout or Venture Air Scout uniform to show that they hold specialist qualifications.

(ii) A Venture Scout is permitted to qualify for and wear the Master Airman badge provided he has satisfied the requirements of the Airman and Senior Airman badges either by gaining these badges as a Scout or by meeting the necessary requirements (excepting Requirement 1 of the Senior Airman badge and Requirements 1 and 2 of the Master Airman badge).

The Service Flash

To be passed under arrangements made by the Scout Leader and awarded by the Patrol Leaders' Council.
A red stripe on a green background with the Arrowhead Badge.

Requirements

1. Either hold the Advanced Scout Standard or have reached the age of fourteen years.

2. Have gained two of the Service group of proficiency badges. A badge from the Interest or Pursuit group may qualify in place of one of these badges if, in addition to holding the badge, you are carrying out regular service under the heading of the badge, e.g. Librarian or Bell Ringer.

3. Have gained one of the Instructor group of proficiency badges or the Ambulance (Service) proficiency badge, provided it has not been gained under requirement 2.

4. Put into practice the training you have received from gaining a Service or Instructor badge by giving regular service over a period of at least three months *after* gaining the badge. An equivalent of one hour a week is the normal standard required.

The Patrol Leader's Training Emblem

To be passed under arrangements made by the Scout Leader.
A blue stripe on a green background with the Arrowhead Badge.

Requirements

Attend a course in Patrol Leader training organised by the Troop or District.

The Senior Patrol Leader's Badge

One narrow and two broad gold bars and the Arrowhead Badge on a green background.
Worn by Senior Patrol Leaders appointed in accordance with *Rule I, 7 iii (b)*.

The Patrol Leader's Badge

Two gold bars and the Arrowhead Badge on a green background.
Worn by Patrol Leaders appointed in accordance with *Rule I, 7 iii (b)*.

The Assistant Patrol Leader's Badge

One gold bar and the Arrowhead Badge on a green background.
Worn by Assistant Patrol Leaders appointed in accordance with *Rule I, 7 iii (b)*.

Method of Wear

Scout Training Badges are worn on the uniform as shown in the illustration on Page 266. Other emblems relevant to Scout uniform are detailed in Uniform on Pages 180–191.

The Venture Scout Training Programme

Rule 14 — Entry to the Venture Scout Unit

Young people may enter the Venture Scout Unit either:

from the Scout Troop, on reaffirming the Scout Promise and acquiring the Venture Scout Membership Badge (See Page 169), for which requirements may be met during the three months prior to entry *(See Rule I, 7 iii (f))*, or on making the Scout Promise and acquiring the Venture Scout Membership Badge as a new Member of the Association. The Venture Scout Membership Badge is the same as the World Membership Badge (See Page 192).

Rule 15 — Venture Scout Awards

Rule 15 i

There are two awards which may be gained in the course of Venture Scout training:
The Venture Award
The Queen's Scout Award

Rule 15 ii

The requirements of these awards may be met in any order convenient to the Venture Scout but all the requirements for the Venture Award must be met before the Queen's Scout Award can be awarded.

Rule 15 iii

Recent achievements in the Scout Troop may be counted towards the requirements of the Venture Award, subject to the approval of the Unit Executive Committee.

Rule 15 iv

(a) The Venture Award is passed under arrangements made by the Unit Executive Committee, which is the awarding authority.

(b) The Queen's Scout Award is passed under similar arrangements but the awarding authority is the District Commissioner who will consult with the Venture Scout Leader and the Unit Executive Committee and interview the Venture Scout informally.

Rule 16

Venture Scouts – Sea and Air Training Badges

Venture Scout training is adult in concept and results from a programme conceived and carried out by the Venture Scouts of the Unit themselves. There is less emphasis on the acquisition of awards and there are no proficiency badges exclusively for Venture Scouts. However, Venture Scouts may qualify for and wear the Coxswain badge and the Master Airman badge (See Pages 154 and 159 respectively) or their respective Instructor badges and they may continue to wear, if entitled, the Chief Scout's Award (See Pages 63–66) until it is replaced by the Venture Award.

The requirements for the Venture Scout Awards appear on Pages 169–175.

Rule 17 Venture Scout Training

Details of the structure of the Venture Scout Unit are given in *Rule I, 7 iv*. Details of the appointment and responsibilities of Leaders and Instructors are given in *Rules I, 10, 11, 13 vii and viii*. Minimum standards for Venture Scout Units are defined in *Rule I, 7 iv (e)*.

Rule 18 Joint Units

Joint Units, as defined in this rule, may be formed. A Joint Unit is one in which registered Venture Scout and Ranger Guide Units amalgamate under joint leadership. Information on the formation of Joint Units is available from the Association's Headquarters.

Rule 19

The Duke of Edinburgh's Award Scheme

Rule 19 i
The Scout Association is an operating authority for the Duke of Edinburgh's Award Scheme.

Rule 19 ii
The assessors for the various sections of the Bronze, Silver and Gold Awards must be approved as follows:
- for the Bronze Award – by the Group Scout Leader;
- for the Silver Award – by the District Commissioner or an Assistant District Commissioner appointed by him for this purpose;
- for the Gold Award – by the County Commissioner or an Assistant County Commissioner appointed by him for this purpose.

Rule 19 iii
On the completion of each stage, the Bronze, Silver and Gold Awards must be authorised by the following Scout Association authorities:
- the Bronze Award – the District Commissioner or an Assistant District Commissioner appointed by him for this purpose;
- the Silver Award – the County Commissioner or an Assistant County Commissioner appointed by him for this purpose;
- the Gold Award – in England, the Channel Islands and the Isle of Man, the Headquarters of The Scout Association;
  – in Northern Ireland, the Northern Ireland Scout Council;
  – in Scotland, Scottish Headquarters;
  – in Wales, the Welsh Scout Council.

Rule 19 iv

Each award has a certificate, a lapel badge and a cloth badge for wear with uniform. Bronze and Silver Awards are presented by the District Commissioner or by a local authority. Gold Award badges are presented locally, but the certificate is normally presented at a reception arranged in one of the Royal Palaces.

Further information about this scheme is to be found in *Scout Training and the Duke of Edinburgh's Award*, published by The Scout Association.

Venture Scout Training Badge and Awards

The Venture Scout Membership Badge

To be passed under arrangements made by the Venture Scout Leader, in consultation with the Unit Executive Committee.

The Arrowhead Badge on a purple background surrounded by a rope in a circle, tied in a reef knot at the bottom.

Requirements

FOR A SCOUT ENTRANT:

Action

1. Take part with members of the Unit in at least one worthwhile activity.

Note: The holder of a Chief Scout's Award who may have been associated with Venture Scouts in obtaining part of Section 1 – Achievement in that Award qualifies for this section.

Understanding

2. Show that you understand the aims and international aspects of the Scout Movement and what is expected of you as a Venture Scout.

Commitment

3. Accept the Scout Promise and Law.

Note: A Scout may qualify for Sections 2 and 3 of the Membership Badge during the three months prior to his transfer from the Scout Troop.

FOR A NEW ENTRANT:

Action

1. Take part in the activities of the Unit on at

least six occasions and during that time take part with other members of the Unit in at least one worthwhile outdoor activity approved by the Unit Executive Committee.

Understanding
2. Show that you understand the aims and international aspects of the Scout Movement and what is expected of you as a Venture Scout.

Commitment
3. Accept the Scout Promise and Law.

The Venture Award

To be passed under arrangements made by the Unit Executive Committee.
A white V with a laurel wreath and an Arrowhead Badge on a brown background.

Requirements

To achieve the Venture Award a Venture Scout must have made personal progress and widened his experience and skill in each of eight sections. Examples of some of the activities possible are given to illustrate the range within each section. Fuller details of possible activities and standards to be reached are to be found in *Venture Scout Programmes* published by The Scout Association.

Outdoors and Environment
– e.g. sports, conservation projects, expeditions, survival training, outdoor pursuits, lightweight camping.

Community Involvement
– e.g. community service, first aid or rescue training, help in Scouting, community relations projects, social work.

Physical Activities
– e.g. hiking, swimming, orienteering, sports

and active pursuits, fitness training, instructing others in such activities.

Creative Pursuits

– e.g. magazine production, photography, interior decorating, tape recording, industrial archaeology, cooking, music.

Relationships with others

– e.g. leadership or introductory courses, work with young, elderly or handicapped, instructing, entertaining, Executive Committee responsibilities, joining planning group for specific project.

Personal Values

– e.g. understanding different faiths, political issues, debating current moral issues, examining local 'pressure groups' and voluntary social organisations.

International Dimension

– e.g. expeditions abroad, foreign cooking, international work camps, overseas aid agencies, projects with immigrant families, foreign visitors, exchange visits.

Design for Living

– e.g. health education, catering, setting up home, marriage guidance, local politics, further education, job opportunities, trade unions.

Notes:

(i) A particular activity may only be counted for one section of the Award.

(ii) Recent achievements gained through the Scout Section may, at the discretion of the Executive Committee, count towards parts of this Award.

(iii) Older Scouts, whilst in the Scout Troop, are encouraged to join with members of the Unit undertaking parts of this Award and can count this experience when they eventually join the Unit. It is intended that most of the Award requirements shall be completed within and as a member of the Venture Scout Unit.

The Queen's Scout Award

To be passed under arrangements made by the Unit Executive Committee and awarded by the District Commissioner after consultation with the Venture Scout Leader and the Unit Executive Committee and after an informal interview with the Venture Scout.
A gold crown with ornamentation on a brown background with a white border.

Requirements

1. Hold the Venture Award.

2. Community – training and involvement.

(a) Undertake training in helping the community in such fields as:

rescue, (e.g. cave, mountain, beach, fire, coastguard, canoe) *or emergency aid services;*

first aid, to the standard of the Adult First Aid Certificate of the St. John Ambulance Association, British Red Cross Society or the Senior Certificate of the St. Andrew's Ambulance Association or, if gained for the Venture Award, to a higher standard;

life saving, qualifying for the Bronze Medallion of the Royal Life Saving Society or, if gained for the Venture Award, for the Award of Merit of the Royal Life Saving Society;

Leader Training in Scouting (General Information Course, three months practical service with the Cub Scout or Scout Section, and Basic Training Course);

specialist training e.g. to help the blind, elderly, mentally or physically handicapped;

specialist activity as an instructor e.g. Canoe Instructor, Sunday School teacher, or F.A. referee;

other forms of community service training approved by Headquarters.

(b) Undertake at least forty-eight hours practical effort to help the community. Depending on the local needs, this may be spread over several months or take a more concentrated form. The service might be one of the following:

in the local community, such as working in a hospital, assisting in the work of your church, helping with handicapped children; helping to run an adventure playground, or a Cycling Proficiency Scheme;

working on conservation projects, such as with the Conservation Corps, or National Trust; helping to restore inland waterways, narrow gauge railways or other forms of industrial archaeology; improving National Parks, camp sites or derelict city areas;

helping in Scouting, for example as a regular instructor with a Cub Scout Pack or Scout Troop, where possible in another Group, and taking appropriate training; helping staff to maintain a permanent camp site or activity centre; running a Group or District magazine for six months; providing specialist skills as an instructor, e.g. in swimming, canoeing or photography, up to Scout proficiency badge standards;

helping with some form of social service or work-camp at home or abroad, arranged by a local authority or voluntary organisation.

3. Pursuit or Interest

Complete (a) or (b)

(a) Reach a reasonable standard in a physical or creative pursuit, sport or hobby. This can be either an entirely new activity or an existing one developed to a higher level of achievement. (Suggestions on standards appropriate are available in the Duke of Edinburgh's Award Handbook, *Programmes*, or from Headquarters.)

(b) Undertake two further items from different areas of the Venture Award. These items must be different from those used to qualify for the Venture Award.

4. Exploration – training and expedition

(a) Carry out suitable training appropriate to the type of expedition you intend to undertake, e.g.:

for an expedition on foot this might include shorter practice hikes, lightweight camping experience, selection of correct clothing and equipment, load carrying, food, cooking, hygiene, map reading and compass work, route planning, leading a party, accident precautions and procedures, expedition first aid.

(b) Plan and undertake an expedition over four/five days in unfamiliar country. This must be approved by the Unit Executive Committee, e.g.:

- ☐ on foot – 80 kilometres (50 miles) in wild country with a small group (at least four in number);
- ☐ by cycle – 240 kilometres (150 miles) including rural areas;
- ☐ by canoe, dinghy, raft or punt –
  80 kilometres (50 miles) on suitable inland waterways or sheltered coastal waters;
- ☐ on horseback – 160 kilometres (100 miles) including bridle paths and trackless sections of wild country.

Notes:

(i) Enterprising expeditions abroad are encouraged. Distance can be varied according to local conditions of climate and terrain, but they must involve the party in careful preparation and physical effort and sustained endeavour in an area unknown to members.

(ii) Mixed expeditions are acceptable, but some reductions may be necessary in the mileage requirements. For general guidance, with joint expeditions involving Ranger Guides, those taking part must follow normal Ranger Guide hike/camp requirements.

(iii) In individual cases where a four/five day expedition is not feasible, then two linked expeditions of shorter duration are permissible, at the discretion of the Unit Executive Committee.

5. Assessment and Interview

On completion of the above requirements, the Venture Scout will discuss these achievements with the Unit Executive Committee and arrange for an informal interview with the District Commissioner to discuss these achievements and future plans. The District Commissioner will receive a report from the Venture Scout Leader, who will have consulted the Unit Executive Committee.

Method of Wear

Venture Scout training badges are worn on the uniform as shown in the illustration on Page 267. Other emblems relevant to Venture Scout uniform are detailed in Uniform on Pages 180–191.

Extension Activities

Rule 20

Extension Activities

The Scout Association offers membership and training to boys with a handicap. There is no special training programme, but the appropriate training will be adjusted to meet the special needs of such members, who may join registered Extension Groups or ordinary Scout Groups as appropriate.

The Training of Leaders

Rule 21   The Religious Policy of The Scout Association as applied to Leaders

The District Commissioner or the County Commissioner as appropriate must satisfy himself that all applicants for leader appointments are fully aware that they will be expected by their personal example to implement the Association's religious policy as defined in *Rule 1 above*.

Rule 22   Leader Training Obligations

Rule 22 i

The acceptance of a Warrant involves an obligation to undertake training appropriate to the appointment for which the Warrant is issued. Training is also available for Instructors, Administrators and Advisers, who do not have the same obligation, but who are encouraged to avail themselves of the training provided.

Rule 22 ii

The retention and renewal of Warrants is dependent on the satisfactory completion of the appropriate training *(See Rules I, 10 ii (c) & I, 10 iv)*.

Rule 22 iii

Cub Scout Instructors should attend a Cub Scout Instructors Course as soon as possible after appointment *(See Rule I, 11 ii (b))*.

Rule 23

Initial Training

Rule 23 i

Initial Training starts immediately upon the appointment of a new Leader. This training is the responsibility of the Assistant District Commissioner (Leader Training).

Rule 23 ii

Initial Training provides practical opportunities, advice and information to help the Leader. It provides an explanation of the Aim and the implementation of the Method of The Scout Association. It includes a General Information meeting for small groups or individuals from one or more Sections which will cover fundamental principles, the structure of Scouting and the responsibilities of leadership. A set of background questions is used to extend the training.

Rule 24

Basic Training

Rule 24 i

All Leaders including Commissioners must complete Basic Training within one year of appointment.

Rule 24 ii

(a) Basic Training is Sectional in character and gives Scouters a grounding in the skills, methods and principles relating to the particular

Section in which they are working. Basic Training is of a minimum duration of 22 hours in two parts separated by at least two months, during which time the Scouters work on assignments in their Group.

(b) Additionally, there are Courses for Group Scout Leaders, Commissioners and Administrators. Assistant District Commissioners may attend a *Training in the District Course* as an alternative. These Courses usually take place over one or two weekends. Assignments are issued at the end of these Courses to extend the training.

(c) At the end of Basic Training, the Basic Training Emblem *(see Rule II, 53 i)* may be worn by those who qualify.

Rule 25 Advanced Training

Rule 25 i

All Section Leaders, Group Scout Leaders, District Scouters and Commissioners must complete Advanced Training within five years of appointment.

Rule 25 ii

(a) The Advanced Training Course continues the training given on the Basic Course. Leaders are given a deeper insight into their work and are equipped with skills and understanding to help them work more effectively. Advanced Courses last a week or take place over three weekends.

(b) Assignments are completed either at the end of a week's course or between the second and third weekends of a three weekend course when a period of at least four months separates the second and third weekends.

(c) In-Service Training begins either at the end of the continuous one week course or after the second weekend of a three weekend course. It will consist of a period of not less than four months, but may run concurrently with the Assignments. The District Commissioner may extend this period if considered necessary. During this period, Scouters continue working with their Group while receiving encouragement and support from the District Commissioner and Assistant District Commissioners. The County Commissioner will arrange for the In-Service Training for Commissioners.

(d) The District Commissioner (the County Commissioner in the case of a Commissioner) may recommend the award of the Advanced Training Award, the Wood Badge, to those who have satisfactorily completed the Advanced Course, Assignments and In-Service Training. The Wood Badge may be worn after confirmation of the Award by the Association's Headquarters *(see Rule II, 53 ii)*.

Rule 26 — Specialist Courses

Courses open to all Scouters are arranged for those wishing to extend their knowledge in particular fields, e.g. water activities, mountaineering.

Rule 27 — Local Education Authorities

Many Local Education Authorities run basic common element courses and specialist activity courses for youth leaders; Scouters are encouraged to participate in such courses.

Uniform

Rule 28 — Protection

The Association's uniforms are protected under the Chartered Associations (Protection of Names and Uniforms) Act, 1929. It is unlawful for persons not entitled as Members of the Association *(See Rule II, 29)* to wear them, except that they may be worn on the stage, in pageants or films, provided that they are not brought into contempt.

Rule 29 — Entitlement

The appropriate uniform, as described in the following Rules, may be worn by all Members of the Association *(See Rule I, 3)*.

Rule 30 — Authority

The correct uniform as defined in these rules should be worn on public occasions specified by appropriate Scouters and Commissioners.

Rule 31 — Safety

In the organisation of all Scouting activities priority is invariably to be given to considerations of safety in specifying what form of dress is to be worn.

Rule 32 — Sheath Knives

Sheath knives may not be worn with uniform.

Rule 33 — Options

The wearing of head dress, scarves or ties and the rolling of sleeves above the elbow are matters for the discretion of the person in charge of the activity. The type of footwear worn with uniform is optional but black or brown shoes should be worn on formal occasions.

Rule 34 — The Kilt

The kilt may be worn as part of the appropriate uniform, subject to the following conditions:

(a) Tartans

In Scotland, all male members who are entitled to wear uniform, except for those who wear Sea and Air Scout uniforms, may wear the kilt of any tartan which they are entitled to wear or of the Scout Tartan.

Elsewhere, Cub Scouts, Scouts and Venture Scouts who are entitled by descent to wear a tartan may wear the kilt and, in Groups in which all Cub Scouts, Scouts and Venture Scouts are so entitled, the holders of appointments may wear the kilt of their own or the Scout Tartan.

Ladies in Scotland and ladies outside Scotland who are associated with a Group in which all Cub Scouts, Scouts and Venture Scouts are entitled to wear the kilt may wear a pleated tartan skirt, in which the tartan is not cut on the cross.

(b) The following items are correct wear with the kilt:

plain leather sporran
plain lovat green stockings
black shoes
head dress
   – Cub Scouts – the Cub Scout cap
   – others – except in Scotland – the Scout beret.

outer jacket, tailored for wear with the kilt.

(c) The Saffron Kilt

In Northern Ireland, all Cub Scouts, Scouts and Venture Scouts and the holders of appointments who are entitled to wear uniform, except for those who wear Sea or Air Scout uniforms, may wear the Saffron Kilt.

Elsewhere, Cub Scouts, Scouts and Venture Scouts who are entitled by descent to do so may wear the Saffron kilt and, in Groups in which all Cub Scouts, Scouts and Venture Scouts are so entitled, the holders of appointments may wear the Saffron Kilt, except for those who wear Sea or Air Scout uniforms.

The Saffron kilt may not be worn in uniform by ladies.

Rule 35　Identifying Scarves and Emblems

Rule 35 i　Name Tapes

The name of the Group, local Venture Scout Unit or District Scout Fellowship may appear in red, green, light blue, white or yellow lettering on a single tape no more than ½ inch deep on a green background. The name of Sea and Air Scout Groups may appear in the same colours, but on a dark blue background.

Rule 35 ii　Group, District and County Badges

Group, District and County badges, bearing distinctive identifying emblems and/or lettering and of any size up to 2 inches deep by 1½ inches wide may be worn after approval by the National Headquarters on the recommendation of the County Commissioner, to whom a drawing or specimen of the design must be submitted.

Rule 35 iii   Scarves

Scarves worn by members of a Scout Group as part of the appropriate uniform must all be of the same colour, chosen by the Group Scouters' Meeting, subject to the approval of the District Commissioner and the District Executive Committee. Groups in the same District should wear scarves of different colours if this is possible.

Rule 35 iv   Woggles

Woggles worn with Cub Scout uniform are of the colour by which the Six is named.

Rule 36

Patrol Names, Patches and Colours

Rule 36 i

The following is the standard list of Patrol names and colours. Each badge is on a green background and bears the relevant silhouette and Patrol colours.

Badger	purple and white
Beaver	blue and yellow
Buffalo	red and white
Bulldog	light blue and brown
Curlew	green
Cobra	orange and black
Eagle	green and black
Falcon	red and orange
Fox	yellow and green
Hawk	pink
Kestrel	royal blue and green
Kingfisher	kingfisher blue

Lion	yellow and red
Otter	brown and white
Owl	blue
Panther	yellow
Peewit	green and white
Raven	black
Sea-gull	light blue and scarlet
Stag	violet and black
Swift	navy blue
Tiger	violet
Wolf	yellow and black
Woodpecker	green and purple

Rule 36 ii

Badges of the following colours, bearing a hexagonal abstract design on a green background, may be used so that any existing Patrol names not included in the list given may be retained or so that new names may be used:

red	lime green
white	yellow
orange	light blue

Rule 37   Cub Scout Uniform

Rule 37 i
Green jersey, round neck, raglan long sleeves *or* green T-shirt
Group scarf and identifying Six woggle
Grey shorts with grey stockings with green garter tabs *or* grey long trousers
Green cap with yellow piping with cloth Arrowhead Badge

Rule 37 ii
Badges and emblems worn with Cub Scout uniform (jersey or T-shirt) are positioned as in the illustration on Page 265.

Rule 38   Scout Uniforms

Rule 38 i
Dark green long sleeved shirt with two pockets without pleats
Group scarf and woggle
Mushroom long trousers without turn-ups
Brown leather belt with buckle bearing the Scout Badge
Green beret with metal Arrowhead Badge

Rule 38 ii   Sea Scouts
Navy blue jersey, with double neck and ribbing at the wrists and waist, with the words *Sea Scouts* embroidered in white on the chest *or* light blue-grey long sleeved shirt with two pockets without pleats.
Group scarf either worn with woggle or tied
Navy blue long trousers without turn-ups
Brown leather belt with buckle bearing the

Scout Badge, worn under the jersey
Sea Scout cap
Lanyard (worn only with Bosun's call)

Rule 38 iii   Air Scouts

Light blue-grey long sleeved shirt with two
pockets without pleats
Group scarf and woggle
Air Force blue-grey long trousers without turn-
ups
Brown leather belt with buckle bearing the
Scout Badge
Air Force blue-grey beret with metal Arrow-
head Badge

Rule 38 iv

Badges and emblems worn with Scout uniforms are positioned as in the illustration on
page 266.

Rule 39   Venture Scout Uniforms

Rule 39 i   Venture Scouts

(a) Venture Scouts – Male

The Venture Scout uniform is the same as the Scout uniform in all respects except that:

Shirt is beige

Dark brown tie *or* the Group scarf and woggle is worn

Green outer garment (optional) may be worn

The Explorer Belt, which is a brown leather belt with a special decorative buckle, may be worn instead of the brown leather belt if the Venture Scout is qualified.

(b) Venture Scouts – Female

Beige long sleeved blouse

Mushroom plain skirt *or* long trousers

Dark brown tie *or* scarf *or* Group scarf and woggle

Brown leather belt with buckle bearing the Scout Badge *or* the Explorer Belt *(See Rule 39 i (a) above)*

No headwear

Green outer garment (optional) may be worn.

Rule 39 ii   Venture Sea Scouts

(a) Venture Sea Scouts – Male

Light blue-grey long sleeved shirt with two pockets without pleats

Black tie *or* Group scarf and woggle

Navy blue long trousers without turn–ups

Brown leather belt with buckle bearing the Scout Badge *or* the Explorer Belt *(See Rule 39 i (a) above)*

Peaked cap with white top and Sea Scout cap badge

Navy blue outer garment (optional) may be worn.

(b) Venture Sea Scouts – Female
Light blue-grey long sleeved blouse
Navy blue plain skirt *or* long trousers
Black tie *or* scarf *or* Group scarf and woggle
Brown leather belt with buckle bearing the
Scout Badge *or* the Explorer Belt *(See Rule 39 i
(a) above)*
No headwear
Navy blue outer garment (optional) may be
worn.

Rule 39 iii   Venture Air Scouts

(a) Venture Air Scouts – Male
Venture Air Scouts wear the same uniform as
Air Scouts, except that:
A light blue tie *or* Group scarf and woggle is
worn
Brown leather belt with buckle bearing the
Scout Badge *or* the Explorer Belt *(See Rule 39 i
(a) above)*
Air Force blue-grey outer garment (optional)
may be worn.

(b) Venture Air Scouts – Female
Light blue-grey long sleeved blouse
Air Force blue-grey plain skirt *or* long trousers
Light blue tie *or* scarf *or* Group scarf and woggle
Brown leather belt with buckle bearing the
Scout Badge *or* the Explorer Belt *(See Rule 39 i
(a) above)*
No headwear
Air Force blue-grey outer garment (optional)
may be worn.

Rule 39 iv

Badges and emblems worn with Venture Scout
uniforms are positioned as in the illustration on
page 267.

Adults' Uniforms

Rule 40 i

(a) Male Scouters and other male adult Members of the Association wear the same uniform as Venture Scouts in *Rule 39 i (a) above* except that:

A green tie or the Group scarf and woggle is worn. The Gilwell scarf may be worn when not with the Group, if so entitled.

A Commissioner may wear the Gilwell scarf instead of the green tie, if so entitled.

A member of the International Fellowship of Former Scouts and Guides may wear a blue scarf with the International Fellowship badge on the scarf.

A jacket matching the trousers may be worn on formal occasions.

(b) Sea Scout Groups

Male adults working in Sea Scout Groups who are entitled to wear uniform under *Rule 29 above* wear the same uniform as Venture Sea Scouts with a reefer jacket if desired instead of the navy blue outer garment (optional).

(c) Air Scout Groups

Male adults working in Air Scout Groups who are entitled to wear uniform under *Rule 29 above* wear the same uniform as Venture Air Scouts with a black tie instead of a light-blue tie or the Group scarf.

Rule 40 ii   Ladies' Uniform

(a) Beige long sleeved blouse and mushroom plain skirt or long trousers or beige one-piece dress of the same basic pattern with short or long sleeves.

Green tie, the Group scarf and woggle or the official ladies' neck brooch *(See Rule II, 46)*. The Gilwell Scarf may be worn when not with the Group, if so entitled. If not entitled to wear a Group scarf or the Gilwell scarf, a lemon scarf may be worn instead of a green tie or the official ladies neck brooch.

A Commissioner may wear the Gilwell scarf instead of the green tie, if so entitled.

A Member of the International Fellowship of Former Scouts and Guides may wear a blue scarf with the International Fellowship badge on the scarf.

Brown leather belt with buckle bearing the Scout Badge (optional with one-piece dress).

Green block-type hat.

Green outer garment (optional). A jacket, matching the skirt or one-piece dress may be worn on formal occasions.

(b) Cub Scout Section

Ladies holding an appointment in the Cub Scout Section wear the uniform as in *Rule 40 ii (a) above* either in the colours described or in green.

(c) Sea Scout Groups

Ladies holding an appointment in a Sea Scout Group wear the uniform as in *Rule 40 ii (a) above* but in the colours worn by Venture Sea Scouts. *(See Rule 39 ii (b) above.)*

(d) Air Scout Groups

Ladies holding an appointment in an Air Scout Group wear the uniform as in *Rule 40 ii (a) above* but in the colours worn by Venture Air Scouts. *(See Rule 39 iii (b) above.)*

Rule 40 iii   Cub Scout Instructors

Cub Scout Instructors wear the appropriate adult uniform. Venture Scouts and Ranger Guides who are Cub Scout Instructors wear their Venture Scout or Ranger Guide uniform.

Rule 40 iv   Ranger Guides and Guiders holding Warrants

Ranger Guides holding Warrants of The Scout Association wear the ladies' uniform as in *Rule 40 ii above* on all Scout occasions. Guiders who are also Scouters may wear their Guider's uniform on all Scout occasions.

Rule 40 v

Badges and emblems worn with adults' uniforms are positioned as in the illustration on page 268.

Rule 41   Bands

Rule 41 i

Scout bands whose membership includes both Scouts and Venture Scouts may wear either Scout or Venture Scout uniform, with badges and emblems as in *Rules II, 41 ii or iii*, and with the following additional items:

White gloves, belt and socks
Lanyard around the shoulder
Protective clothing for drummers
Drum Major's sash and/or cords
'Orderly Serjeant's' plain sash or white music pouch.

Rule 41 ii

If Venture Scout uniform is worn, a green tie may be worn instead of the brown and Scouts may wear only their Scout Badge and the Progress Badge to which they are entitled.

Rule 41 iii

If Scout uniform is worn, Venture Scouts may wear only their Membership Badge and the Venture or Queen's Scout Award badge if entitled.

Badges and Awards

Rule 42   Sources of Supply

All Membership badges, proficiency, progress and training award badges must be obtained through County or District Badge Secretaries and from no other source.

Rule 43   Protection

The badges and emblems in use by The Scout Association are protected as defined in *Rule I, 91*.

Rule 44   The World Membership Badge

Rule 44 i

The World Membership Badge is the symbol of membership of World Scouting and of The Scout Association as a part of World Scouting. It is the property of the World Scout Bureau and it may only be used or worn as permitted in these rules.

Rule 44 ii

The two forms of the World Membership Badges are:

(a) for wear with uniform – made of embroidered or woven cloth, with the design as illustrated on page 19 on a purple background;

(b) for wear with ordinary clothes by Members of the Association – made of metal to the same design, pattern and colour.

Rule 45 The Arrowhead Badge

Rule 45 i

The Arrowhead Badge is the symbol of The Scout Association and is part of its armorial bearings.

Rule 45 ii

The Arrowhead Badge is worn:
- on head dress, by Cub Scouts (cloth);
- on head dress by all Scouts, Venture Scouts, adult Members of the Association entitled under *Rule 29 above* to wear uniform, except for Sea and Venture Sea Scouts and adults working in Sea Scout Groups (metal);
- on activity or special garments (e.g. anoraks or track suits), working rig and outer garments, in the activities dress pattern of the badge.

Rule 46 Ladies' Neck Brooch

The brooch worn by ladies in uniform, as in *Rule 40 ii above*, is a yellow metal badge incorporating the Arrowhead Badge.

Rule 47   Recognised Groups

Except for Cub Scouts, all members of Groups which are recognised by the Royal Navy or the Royal Air Force wear the appropriate R.N. or R.A.F. Recognition Badge.

Rule 48   Scout Wings

Rule 48 i   Scout Wings for Flight Training

These may be worn by any Venture Scout or adult leader who has met the following requirements:

made three solo flights in a glider, thus gaining the A Badge of the British Gliding Association (minimum age 16 years);

or

made a solo flight in a balloon (minimum age 17 years)

or

made a solo flight in a powered aircraft (minimum age 17 years).

Rule 48 ii   Scout Wings for Canopy Training

These may be worn by any Venture Scout or adult leader who has met the following requirements:

made eight parachute jumps from a powered aircraft (minimum age 16 years)

or

obtained category B of the British Association of Parascending Clubs proficiency scheme. The twenty-five flights are to include at least five circuits on a self inflating wing canopy (minimum age 16 years).

Note: Only one of these badges may be worn on uniform.

Rule 49

The Duke of Edinburgh's Award Badges

Cloth badges of the Duke of Edinburgh's Award are worn on uniform by Scouts and Venture Scouts who are entitled to wear them. In the case of the Gold Award only, the badge may be worn on uniform by adults so entitled until they reach the age of 25 years.

Rule 50

The Queen's Scout Award Badge

The cloth badge of the Queen's Scout Award may be worn on uniform by those qualified until they reach the age of 25 years.

Rule 51

Occasional Badges worn with Uniform

Badges and emblems authorised from time to time by the Association's Headquarters, including those of organisations entitled to be registered as sponsoring organisations, must be worn as directed by the Association's Headquarters. If authorised for temporary wear in connection with a special gathering, camp, event or Group Anniversary such badges must not be worn after a period of four weeks from the time of the conclusion of the occasion. Badges for wear by Members of a Group, a District or County must be recommended by the County Commissioner to whom a drawing or specimen of the design must be submitted. The Union Flag may be worn on uniform when going overseas and for up to one year on return.

Rule 52   Badges of other Organisations

The following badges of other organisations may be worn with uniform:
- ☐ the junior and senior proficiency badges of the St. John and the St. Andrew's Ambulance Associations;
- ☐ the British Red Cross Society Junior First Aid and Public Service Arm Badges;
- ☐ the cloth badge of the Royal Life Saving Society;
- ☐ the life-saving medals of the Order of St. John and the Royal Humane Society, together with their ribbons.

Rule 53   Leader Training Awards

Rule 53 i   The Basic Training Emblem

Leaders who have completed Basic Training *(See Rule 24 ii above)* may wear the Basic Training Emblem with uniform. This emblem consists of a tie slide or pin; a brooch is available for ladies. The Gilwell Woggle may be worn by Leaders who wear their Group scarf.

Rule 53 ii   The Advanced Training Award (Wood Badge)

The Advanced Training Award is the Wood Badge. It is worn on a leather thong around the neck. It may be worn with the Basic Training Emblem. Leaders holding the Wood Badge may also wear the Gilwell Scarf when they are not with their Scout Groups.

Decorations and Awards

Rule 54

Applications for Decorations and Awards

Applications for Scout decorations and awards must be initiated by a District or County Commissioner. Application forms, as listed below, detail the necessary qualifications and the administrative procedure and may be obtained by these Commissioners or by District or County Secretaries from the Association's Headquarters.

Form H – Application for Award for Gallantry.

Form I – Application for Award for Good Service to the Movement.

Form J – Application for 'Cornwell Scout' Badge.

Form K – Application for Award for Meritorious Conduct.

Form L – Application for Long Service Decoration.

Rule 55 The Cornwell Scout Badge

The Cornwell Scout Badge is awarded in respect of pre-eminently high character and devotion to duty, together with great courage and endurance. It is reserved exclusively to Members of the Association under the age of eighteen who have an outstanding record of service and efficiency. It may be worn after the holder has attained the age of eighteen. Both the bronze badge and the emblem of the same design may be worn. *See also Rule II, 61* for method of wear.

Rule 56 Awards for Gallantry

Rule 56 i Eligibility

Awards for gallantry are granted at the discretion of the Association's Headquarters to Cub Scouts, Scouts, Venture Scouts, Groups or local Venture Scout Units collectively, Scouters, Instructors, Administrators, Advisers and Honorary Scouters.

Rule 56 ii Gallantry Awards

(a) The Bronze Cross

The Bronze Cross, with a red ribbon, is the highest award of the Association for gallantry, granted for special heroism or action in the face of extraordinary risk.

(b) The Silver Cross

The Silver Cross, with a blue ribbon, is awarded for gallantry in circumstances of considerable risk.

(c) The Gilt Cross

The Gilt Cross, with a blue and red vertically patterned ribbon, is awarded for gallantry in circumstances of moderate risk.

(d) A Bar may be awarded to the holder of any gallantry award for further acts of gallantry in circumstances of similar risk.

(e) Chief Scout's Commendation

A Chief Scout's Commendation for gallantry, with a blue and white knot cloth emblem, may be awarded for acts of gallantry in circumstances of less risk than that specified for the award of a Cross or Bar.

Rule 57   Awards for Meritorious Conduct

Rule 57 i   Eligibility

Awards for meritorious conduct are granted at the discretion of the Association's Headquarters, to the same categories of recipients as are eligible for gallantry awards as in *Rule 56 i above*, for conduct involving a high degree of courage, endurance, initiative or devotion to duty, often under suffering, without necessarily involving any element of risk.

Rule 57 ii   Meritorious Conduct Awards

(a) The Medal of Meritorious Conduct

The Medal of Meritorious Conduct, on a green ribbon with a red vertical stripe, is the highest award for meritorious conduct. A Bar may be awarded to the holder for further acts of comparable conduct.

(b) The Certificate of Meritorious Conduct

The Certificate of Meritorious Conduct, with a green and white knot cloth emblem, is awarded for meritorious conduct of a moderate standard.

(c) Chief Scout's Commendation

A Chief Scout's Commendation, with a green and blue knot cloth emblem, is awarded for meritorious conduct of a lower standard than that for which the Medal or Certificate are awarded.

Rule 58 Awards for Good Service

Rule 58 i Eligibility

Awards for good service are granted at the discretion of the Association's Headquarters to adult Members or Associate Members of the Association and, exceptionally, to others who have given valuable service to Scouting over a considerable period.

Rule 58 ii Good Service Awards

(a) The Silver Wolf

The Silver Wolf, worn on a green and yellow ribbon around the neck, is the unrestricted gift of the Chief Scout, awarded for service of the most exceptional nature.

(b) The Silver Acorn

The Silver Acorn, worn on an orange ribbon around the neck, is awarded for specially distinguished service. A Bar to the award, denoted by the substitution of an orange ribbon with a green stripe, may be awarded for further distinguished service.

(c) The Medal of Merit
The Medal of Merit, with a green ribbon, is awarded after a period of not less than ten years of outstanding service. A Bar, with a green ribbon with a vertical orange stripe, may be awarded after not less than five years of further outstanding service.

(d) Chief Scout's Commendation
A Chief Scout's Commendation, with a white and yellow knot cloth badge and a brooch of similar design, is awarded for good service over a considerable period.

Rule 59

The Long Service Decoration

Rule 59 i   Eligibility
The Long Service Decoration is granted to adult Members of the Association who have given fifteen years service while holding appointments. The service need not be continuous.

Rule 59 ii
The decoration consists of a cloth badge with a white knot.

Rule 60

Emblems and Certificates of Awards

When the insignia of a Scout decoration or award is not worn with uniform, it is represented by an emblem having a knot design in appropriate colours. The award of a Bar to any decoration is indicated by the Arrowhead

Badge superimposed over the centre of the knot design. The Arrowhead is green for the Bar to the Silver Acorn, gold for all other awards. All awards are accompanied by a certificate.

Rule 61 Method of Wear

Rule 61 i Position on Uniform

Scout decorations (except the Silver Wolf and the Silver Acorn and its Bar) and the emblems corresponding to them are worn immediately above the right breast pocket flap, or in the same position on the ladies' uniform, in the following order from the wearer's left to right:

Awards for gallantry, meritorious conduct, good service, long service decorations.

The Cornwell Scout Badge is worn above this line of emblems.

Rule 61 ii Precedence

Only the highest award received for good service and its emblem may be worn.

Rule 61 iii Collective Awards

Where a collective award for gallantry or meritorious conduct is made to a Group or local Venture Scout Unit, this may be attached to the Group Flag at the hoist.

Rule 61 iv Other Decorations

Ribbons of King's and Queen's medals, war medals, decorations and orders, ribbons of decorations conferred by foreign governments and decorations conferred by foreign Scout Associations may be worn with uniform. Such ribbons are worn above the left breast pocket flap or in the same position on the ladies' uniform.

Rule 62

Other Badges worn with Uniform

The badge of the International Fellowship of Former Scouts and Guides may be worn by members of a District Scout Fellowship who are also Members of the Association *(See I, 84 ii)*. When in uniform, they wear the cloth badge, above the right breast pocket and above any decorations worn there. They may also wear the metal lapel badge when in ordinary clothes.

Rule 63

Badges not worn with Uniform

Rule 63 i   The Associate's Badge

The Associate's Badge is a metal lapel badge, which may be worn by Associate Members of the Association, including members of a District Scout Fellowship who are not Members of the Association. Members of Group Councils may wear the Associate's Badge.

Rule 63 ii   The Thanks Badge

(a) The Thanks Badge is the means of expressing the appreciation of the Association to those who are not active Members but who have been of service to Scouting. The badge may be presented by a Cub Scout, Scout or Venture Scout or a Leader provided that the permission of the District Commissioner has been obtained. It is for wear with ordinary clothes and does not confer Membership or Associate

Membership of the Association on the recipient.

(b) If the person to whom the Thanks Badge is presented is connected with Scouting in another District, the approval of the Commissioner of that District must also be obtained.

Rule 64   Mourning

A black crepe band two inches wide may be worn on the left arm above the elbow to denote mourning.

Ceremonial

Rule 65   The Scout Motto

The Scout Motto is *Be Prepared*.

Rule 66   Flags

Rule 66 i   Permitted Flags

(a) The following flags may be used:
- □ **The National Flag:** on land, the Union Flag; at sea, the Red Ensign
- □ **Group, District and County Flags**
- □ **Patrol Flags**

(b) Groups recognised by the Royal Navy may use a Red Ensign defaced with the Scout Badge surmounted by an Admiralty Crown in the fly. Royal Air Force Recognised Groups use a light blue pennant bearing the Arrowhead Badge, the Scout Motto and the Royal Air Force roundel in the fly.

Rule 66 ii   Pennants

Green camp pennants, Venture Scout pennants

and blue Scout pennants may be used as appropriate to suitable occasions. The blue pennant is the burgee to be flown with the Royal Navy Recognised Group Ensign.

Rule 66 iii   Scout Flags

(a) Flags used by Scout Groups must be of uniform size, mounted on poles bearing the Arrowhead Badge as a mount and must bear the Scout Badge, consisting of a white Arrowhead to the approved specification on a purple circle, and the Scout motto. In addition, they may only bear the words *Cub Scouts, Scouts* or *Venture Scouts* and the Group title.

(b) Flags used by Scout Districts and Counties are of a similar design and may bear the name and emblem of the District or County in addition to the Scout Badge as described in *Rule 66 iii (a) above* and the Scout motto.

(c) Colours
The colours to be used in Group flags, except in Scotland, are as follows:

- □ Cub Scout Packs – white lettering on a yellow background
- □ Scout Troops – white lettering on a green background
- □ Air Scout Troops or Venture Air Scout Units – yellow lettering on a light blue background
- □ Sea Scout Troops or Venture Sea Scout Units – white lettering on a navy blue background
- □ Venture Scout Units – white lettering on a bronze background.

(d) In Scotland, Scout flags are matriculated by the Lord Lyon King of Arms and consist of the St. Andrew's Cross at the hoist with green fly and the Arrowhead Badge in yellow. Area flags have the name of the Area in a bar above the badge in the colour of the Area.

The colours in Group flags in Scotland are:
Cub Scout Packs – yellow background with the badge in green and with yellow lettering on

green bars.

Scout Troops – green background with the badge in yellow and with the name of the Troop in black lettering on yellow bars.

Venture Scout Units – green background with the badge in yellow and with lettering in black on a dark brown background.

Note: Awards for gallantry or meritorious conduct made to Groups or local Venture Scout Units collectively may be attached to the Group Flag at the hoist in accordance with Rule 61 iii above.

Rule 67

Scout Bands

Rule 67 i   Formation of Scout Bands

(a) Scout Bands may be formed by Groups or Districts. The Group Scout Leader or the District Commissioner as appropriate must ensure that members of such bands take an active part in other Troop or Unit activities and that their progress through the training programme does not suffer as a result of band obligations.

(b) Mixed Scout and Guide bands may be formed with the approval of the Commissioners concerned.

Rule 67 ii   Standards and Conduct

(a) Scout Bands will be inspected annually by the County Band Adviser where such an appointment is made. The County Band Adviser will give approval for the band to play in public according to the following standards:

☐ the minimum number of members in the band must be twelve;

☐ the band must have suitable accommodation for practice in which it may train and rehearse without causing a nuisance to the public *(See also Rule II, 67 iii);*

- the Scout Council concerned must ensure that finance adequate to the maintenance and replacement of instruments is available;
- the band must have a bandmaster;
- the band must maintain a good standard of performance and have a reasonable repertoire.

(b) The County Band Adviser will send a copy of his report to the Group Scout Leader, the District Commissioner and the County Commissioner. If the report is satisfactory, he will issue a certificate, signed by himself and the County Commissioner and will inform the Association's Headquarters that the band is permitted to play in public for a period of twelve months from the date of inspection.

(c) If the report is not satisfactory, the County Band Adviser will inform the bandmaster, the District and County Commissioners that the band is not permitted to play in public until such time as they may reach the required standard.

Rule 67 iii Avoidance of Nuisance

Bands must be so conducted as to avoid nuisance to the public and must not play when passing churches, hospitals or houses in which it is known that there is illness. Local government bye-laws in regard to the conduct of bands and the playing of individual instruments must be observed.

See Rule 41 above concerning uniforms for bands.

Scout Ceremonies

Rule 68 — Scout Ceremonies

In the conduct of normal Scouting activities, only those ceremonies described in the Association's handbooks should be used.

Rule 69 — Presentations

Rule 69 i

All awards should be presented as soon as possible after they have been gained.

Rule 69 ii   The Chief Scout's Award

The Chief Scout's Award badge should be presented by the District Commissioner or an Assistant District Commissioner at a Group occasion. The certificate should ideally be presented by a person of standing such as the Lord Lieutenant of a County or the County Commissioner at a suitable event or reception arranged for this purpose.

Rule 69 iii   The Queen's Scout Award

The Queen's Scout Award badge should be presented by the County Commissioner or his delegate at a Group or District occasion. Whenever possible, Queen's Scouts should also attend a special reception to receive their Royal Certificate from the Chief Scout. When this is not possible, the Royal Certificate should be presented at a suitable occasion by a person of appropriate standing such as the Chief Commissioner or the Lord Lieutenant of a County.

Notes:

(i) See Rule 19 above concerning the presentation of the Duke of Edinburgh's Award.

(ii) See Rule I, 10 iii concerning the presentation of Warrants.

Rule 70

The Scout Sign and Salute

Rule 70 i   The Scout Sign

The Scout Sign, as shown left, is made during the making or reaffirming of the Scout Promise and the Cub Scout Promise and at no other time.

Rule 70 ii   The Scout Salute

The Scout Salute, as shown left, is made only by Members of the Association in uniform as a greeting on formal Scouting occasions, as a mark of respect at the hoisting of National flags, at the playing of National Anthems, to uncased colours, Scout flags and to funerals.

Rule 70 iii

On all parades of a public nature, other than in church, the leader calls his party to the alert and he alone salutes.

Activity Rules

Rule 71   General

Scout programmes are by their very nature practical and involve activity in the widest sense. For all activities and games there is a requirement for common sense and responsibility. When Scouters are responsible for young people they must act in the same way as a sensible parent, taking responsible care for the safety and health of those in their charge. Where activities involve going away from home or are of an adventurous nature, thus providing an element of risk, it is necessary to provide rules.

All activities involve risk, but with good training, proper equipment and responsible leadership, these risks can be minimised to provide adventure and fun for all Members of the Movement. When Members or units of the Association use their personal or unit transport on activities, they should be aware of the current regulations affecting motor transport. Guidance can be obtained from Headquarters. This Section of *Policy, Organisation and Rules* sets out to cover these main fields of activity. Where an activity is itself governed by a National Authority, which has its own standards and rules, the Association has, wherever possible, adopted these rules.

There are, however, some rules which apply to all activities and these are set out below.

Rule 71 i   Application
The following rules apply to all activities carried out anywhere in the world.

Rule 71 ii   Leadership

(a) All participants in activities must have received the proper training, be suitably equipped and briefed about the nature and scope of the activity, be of an appropriate age and be subject to authorised leadership. The District Commissioner is normally responsible for authorising the leadership of these activities. For particular events and activities, authorisation will be granted by a Headquarters Commissioner or a County Commissioner.

(b) During an activity, provided that it forms a part of a properly planned training programme, Venture Scouts, Instructors or Leaders over the age of eighteen years, who have been authorised to lead an activity in accordance with these rules, may delegate responsibility to another Member of the Association or authorised helper who may lead and exercise full control over parties of Cub Scouts, Scouts or Venture Scouts. Such delegation should only be made to those who have sufficient training, experience and maturity of judgement to exercise responsible leadership in the anticipated conditions and as provided in these rules.

Rule 71 iii   Communication

(a) When an activity takes Members of the Association away from their home area, it is important to have a link with the home base (in the case of transport breaking down, illness, etc.). This person should be able to get in touch with parents or next of kin, when it is necessary for them to be informed.

(b) When adventurous activities are taking place away from the home area, each party should always appoint a 'Home Contact' in the home area, (e.g. Group Scout Leader, Group Secretary), preferably not related to any member of the party. The 'Home Contact' must be in possession of the names and addresses of the next of kin of each member of the party, and know how to contact the party, the host and home Scout authorities.

Rule 71 iv   Accident Procedure

(a) Accidents to individuals and/or involving damage to property must be reported. In the case of an accident to an individual, the leader of the party is responsible for alerting the appropriate rescue services and/or informing the 'Home Contact'. The 'Home Contact', when informed of the accident, must advise:

☐ the next of kin;

☐ the Public Relations Officer at Headquarters, whose telephone number is 01-584 7030, or after office hours 01-953 1393. In Scotland, Scottish Headquarters should be informed, telephone number 031-226 7375, or after office hours 031-332 5348. Contact with the news media should not be initiated by a member of the party, before receiving approval from the above authority. In exceptional cases, the media representatives may arrive before it is possible to contact these authorities, in which case care must be taken when making statements;

☐ the host Scout authority;

☐ the home Scout authority.

(b) The home Scout authority should ensure that:

☐ a clear communications link is maintained between next of kin and the leader at the site of the accident;

☐ appropriate arrangements are made for the return of the party as necessary;

☐ in cases of serious injury, every assistance should be given to enable the next of kin to visit the casualty.

(c) The host Scout authority should maintain contact with the leader concerned with the accident and with the rescue services involved, and:

☐ offer any support or guidance necessary;
☐ ensure that a clear communications link is maintained with home authorities and Headquarters;
☐ make an immediate assessment of the situation, and report to Headquarters.

(d) As soon as possible after the accident, the host Scout authority must prepare a detailed report of the accident and rescue – incorporating information regarding rescue services and other assistance obtained – together with any observations relating to the effectiveness of the communication system, and submit copies to both Headquarters and home County Commissioner. This report should not be concerned to apportion responsibility but should aim to provide those essential facts which will help in providing useful guidelines relating to similar occurrences.

(e) The leader of the party or a responsible member must, without delay, prepare a detailed report of the accident and submit it to his District Commissioner.

(f) The home District Commissioner, in conjunction with the leader of the party or other responsible person, will produce a full confidential report relating to authorisation, training, equipment, briefing and leadership of the party involved, together with their observations relating to the sequence of events and possible causes of the accident. This report will be submitted to the home County Commissioner, who will forward it to his Headquarters accompanied by his own observations relating to the circumstances, details of the County support for education and training in respect of such activities, and, as appropriate, any recommendations he intends to implement in the light of experience gained.

Rule 71 v   Over-riding Controls

The County or District Commissioner of the area where activities take place, or their representatives, have an over-riding authority:
☐ to ensure that all participants in these activities observe the requirements of these rules;
☐ if, in his view, it is essential in the interest of safety, to direct that any particular activity shall be postponed, stopped or cancelled.

Rule 71 vi   Insurance

Non-compliance with these Activity Rules can adversely affect a Member's insurance cover.

Rule 72   Activities in the Air

Rule 72 i   Access to Airfields

(a) Before any Member of the Association proceeds on to any private, civil or Service airfield, the permission of the controlling body of the airfield must be obtained.

(b) Instruction must be given to any individual or party proceeding on to an airfield in the following:
☐ the general layout of the airfield, with special reference to runways in use, taxi-ing areas, glider-launching and cable-dropping areas and safe areas for spectators;
☐ the hazards of jet intakes and exhausts, propellers, ejection seats, explosive canopies, glider cables, parascending lines and aviation fuels.

Note: These rules do not apply when visits to civil airports are confined to the spectators' enclosure; or to Service establishments on an open day when using the public enclosures.

Rule 72 ii Flying and Gliding

(a) Any Member of the Association engaging in any flying activity must be given prior instruction in:

□ the use of the aircraft safety harness and other safety equipment;

□ the purpose of the flight, the sensations likely to be experienced and the method of clearing the ears on the descent.

(b) Members of the Association must not fly in a powered aircraft that is piloted by a private pilot who has less than 100 hours flying time as a Captain of an aircraft.

(c) Members of the Association may only fly as passengers in a glider piloted by a pilot who holds the recommendation for passenger carrying from the Chief Flying Instructor of the Gliding Club concerned.

Rule 72 iii Hang Gliding

Hang gliding is not an approved activity for Members of the Association.

Rule 72 iv Parachuting

Members of the Association over the age of sixteen years may take part in parachuting, using the standards and controls laid down by the British Sport Parachuting Association.

Rule 72 v Parascending

Members of the Association over the age of fourteen years may take part in the sport of parascending, using the standards and under the control of a qualified Instructor of the British Association of Parascending Clubs.

Rule 73

Camping and Expeditions

The following rules apply to hikes, camps and expeditions, and include journeys by cycle, motor cycle, car, canoe or boat.

Rule 73 i   Camping Areas

A list of District, County and National camping areas in the United Kingdom is published annually and a confidential list of sites and areas unsuitable for use by Members of the Association is issued annually to District Commissioners. Both lists can be bought by Scouters from Headquarters.

Rule 73 ii   Camping

(a) Every Scouter leading or organising a camp must have a sound knowledge of the Association's policy and principles relating to camping as set out in the Association's publication *Scout Camping*.

(b) The District Commissioner is responsible for the standard of camping in his District and for Scouts from his District, as defined in these rules, and must give his permission for a camp to be held.

(c) Scout and Venture Scout camps of five nights duration or longer must be approved by the home District Commissioner to whom the Scouter responsible must submit form PC, together with the registration fee at least two months before the date of the commencement of the camp.

(d) Scout and Venture Scout camps of four nights duration or less may be arranged without formal application on form PC. The arrangements for such camps must be approved by the District Commissioner or by a Scouter in the Group nominated by the District Commissioner. The Scout Leader or Venture Scout Leader, as appropriate, must know of the arrangements in case of enquiries in the event of an emergency. A means of identification as a Member of the Association should be carried.

(e) When it is intended to visit a site or area frequently during the year, a general notice should be given to the host District Commissioner.

(f) Sleeping bags or blankets must be provided in sufficient numbers to enable each person in camp to make up a separate bed.

(g) Cub Scouts may only be allowed to camp with Scouts and Venture Scouts with the consent of the District Commissioner, but a Cub Scout working for, or holding, the Link Badge, may take part in a camp with Scouts, provided that the camp is under adult leadership or is at a permanent camp site under supervision.

(h) Additional rules for Cub Scout holidays are shown in *Rule II, 73 iii.*

(i) Where members of a Pack, Troop or Unit have been the subject of an unsatisfactory report, the home District Commissioner may require special conditions to be met until he is satisfied that standards have improved to his satisfaction.

Rule 73 iii   Cub Scout Holidays

(a) The leader in charge of a holiday which takes Cub Scouts away overnight must hold a Pack Holiday Certificate.

(b) When organising a holiday for Cub Scouts, the leader must:

☐ obtain the permission of the home District Commissioner to make preliminary arrangements at least two months before the date of the proposed holiday and before any intimation is given to the Cub Scouts or their parents;

Note: If the leader has no previous experience of being in charge of a holiday, or if a holiday led by the same person has been the subject of an unsatisfactory report, the permission of the home District Commissioner must be obtained in writing at least three months before the date of the proposed holiday;

☐ inspect the facilities to be used and be satisfied with the adequacy of the cooking facilities, water supplies and sanitation;

☐ submit a completed form PC, with the appropriate registration fee to the home District Commissioner at least two months before the commencement of the holiday, supported by a programme for wet and dry weather.

(c) Apart from the leader in charge of the holiday, there must be one adult to every six Cub Scouts.

(d) When organising a holiday for Cub Scouts under canvas, *Rules 73 ii (a) and 73 iii (a), (b) and (c) above* apply, together with the following special requirements:

☐ some form of alternative, clean and suitable accommodation, large enough for the whole party of Cub Scouts, must be readily available within walking distance of the site for use in the event of bad weather;

☐ the leader of the camp must have his Pack Holiday Certificate endorsed to the effect that he has had practical experience in camping as a helper at a Cub Scout holiday under canvas.

(e) When Cub Scouts camp with Scouts or Venture Scouts, *Rule 73 ii (g) above* applies.

(f) When intending to take Cub Scouts abroad, *Rule II, 73 v (a)* applies.

Rule 73 iv Expeditions

(a) When expeditions are planned away from the home area, but are to be based upon a stati-

base or camp, *Rule 73 ii above* applies.

(b) Cub Scout expeditions are a normal part of the Cub Scout programme and are usually of only a day's duration. Where Cub Scout expeditions are for a longer period, *Rule 73 iii above* applies.

(c) For Scout and Venture Scout expeditions of four nights duration or less *Rule 73 ii (d) above* applies.

(d) Parties of Scouts or Venture Scouts intending to travel by land or water through a number of Scout Counties over a period of five nights or longer must obtain the permission of the home District Commissioner, although no form PC is required. The County Secretaries of the Scout Counties concerned should be informed of the proposed itinerary.

(e) When expeditions take Members of the Association away from their home area, *Rule 71 iii above* applies.

Rule 73 v   Visits Abroad

(a) In special circumstances, the Association's Headquarters may give permission for Cub Scout Holidays abroad. Applications must be made well in advance and must be accompanied by a recommendation from the District Commissioner.

(b) Visits or camps abroad by Scouts, Venture Scouts or Scouters must have the recommendation of the District Commissioner and must be approved on behalf of Headquarters, by an Assistant County Commissioner (International) or a County International Adviser, to whom a form PC (Abroad) must be submitted. If there is no such County appointment, the form PC (Abroad), with the District Commissioner's recommendation, should be sent to Headquarters.

(c) The leader in charge of a visit or camp abroad is advised to obtain from parents the power to give permission for medical treatment etc., as is normally required to be given by a parent. See also *Rule 71 iii (a) above.*

(d) The leader in charge of boating and canoeing activities abroad must apply the appropriate rules, classifying the waters as defined in *Rule II, 75 iii (d)*. In cases of doubt, the County Water Activities Committee should be consulted.

Rule 73 vi   Visitors to the United Kingdom

Invitations to Scouts and Scouters from abroad to visit or camp in the United Kingdom should not be confirmed until approval has been obtained from the District Commissioner. The Assistant County Commissioner (International) or the County International Adviser, if there is such a County appointment, should also be informed.

Rule 74   Activities on the Land

Rule 74 i   Caving

Caving should be carried out using the standards and controls outlined in the National Caving Code, available from Headquarters.

Rule 74 ii   Moors, Hills and Mountains

It is generally recognised that the main reason for hill walking accidents is that those taking part underestimate the small but dangerous hills, and do not take into account weather conditions that are likely to be met. Additionally preparation, training and equipment are often inadequate.

(a) Members of the Association taking part in activities on moors, hills or mountains should work within the current Code of Practice as set out in *Safety on Mountains* published by the British Mountaineering Council, accepted by the Mountaineering Council for Scotland, and available from Headquarters.

(b) The home District Commissioner is responsible for authorising activities on moors, hills and mountains. He should seek appropriate advice where necessary. Advice is available from the Mountain Advisers in both the home and host areas or from Headquarters.

(c) Before a party sets out for activities on moors, hills and mountains it must have:

- received adequate training;
- a leader with the necessary experience;
- the appropriate equipment;
- taken advice, appropriate to experience and local knowledge.

(d) These rules apply to all mountainous, and non-mountainous areas, at home and abroad, offering little protection against wind/rain/cold/snow during inclement weather conditions.

(e) The size of the party should be dictated by the nature of the activity and the safety factors involved.

(f) A 'Home Contact' must be appointed, in accordance with *Rule 71 iii above*, when activities are taking place away from the home area. Additionally, each party should leave word of its route, and proposed time of return, with a responsible person in the host area (e.g. Youth Hostel Warden, Police, etc.). That person should also be given details of how to contact the 'Home Contact' in an emergency.

(g) In the event of an accident, *Rule 71 iv above* applies.

Rule 74 iii   Rock Climbing

Rock climbing should be carried out in accordance with *Rule 74 ii above*, and in accordance with the guidance laid down by the British Mountaineering Council.

Rule 74 iv   Skiing

Skiing should be carried out using the standards and controls laid down by the National Ski Federation of Great Britain.

Rule 75 Activities on the Water

Rule 75 i   Boat Certificates

(a) Group Scout Leaders and others responsible for operating any boats, owned by or on long term loan to a Member or unit of the Association, must ensure that they are inspected annually by a person appointed by the County Water Activities Committee.

(b) If in sound condition, a Boat Certificate, on the form provided by the Association's Headquarters will be issued, showing the period of its validity and the classifications of water upon which it may be used. Scout Registration Badges will be issued at the same time; these will be displayed on either side of the bow. On canoes, these will be displayed on the deck forward and aft.

(c) Where it is intended that a cruising vessel will proceed over 15 miles offshore, *Rule II, 75 vii* applies.

(d) In the case of other boats, the Scouter in charge of the activity must satisfy himself that the boat is seaworthy for the purpose for which it is to be used.

(e) In all cases, the Scouter in charge of the activity must make certain that the boat carries all necessary equipment, that it is not overloaded and not so stowed that its free working will be hindered.

(f) A tender to a vessel as defined in *Rule II, 75 xvi*, may be issued with its own Boat Certificate, or may be included in the Certificate of the parent vessel.

Rule 75 ii   Charge Certificates

(a) There are three types of Charge Certificate:

    (i)   The Charge Certificate

    (ii) An Authorising Charge Certificate

    (iii) A Class A Mates' Certificate.

(b) The Charge Certificate authorises a person to take sole command of a vessel, which is not under further supervision, except in Class A waters.

Note: This does not override the Association's other rules, including the need to canoe in groups of at least three.

(c) An Authorising Charge Certificate holder may authorise someone who does not hold a Charge Certificate to take command or act as mate of a vessel in waters for which the Authorising Charge Certificate is valid.

(d) A Class A Mates' Certificate, only applies to sailing, powerboating and rowing in Class A waters.

(e) A Charge Certificate need not be held when undertaking water activities on Class C waters.

(f) Charge Certificates are issued by examiners appointed by County Water Activities Committees.

(g) Before any Charge Certificate is granted, the examiner must satisfy himself that:

☐ the person who wishes to receive the Certificate holds the qualifications of technical skill and theoretical knowledge as defined in the tables shown under each activity in these rules;

☐ the person applying for the Certificate is a suitable person to hold the particular Certificate and fully understands the responsibilities it carries and the limits of his authority;

☐ the person applying for the Certificate must have a knowledge of the waters for which the Certificate (or an endorsement to an existing Certificate) is required. He should appreciate local hazards, limits of operation, etc.

Note: In many cases a detailed knowledge may not be required, but rather an understanding of the type of hazard to be expected, local bye-laws and contacts for detailed information when necessary.

(h) Where comparable or higher qualifications than those stipulated in these rules, are held, the advice of the County Water Activities Committee should be sought. If there is any doubt the matter should be referred to Headquarters.

(i) Certificates will be valid for a maximum of three years, but may be renewed by a Charge Certificate Examiner, for further periods of up to three years.

(j) Members of the Association under the age of eighteen may act under the authority of their Charge Certificate only after obtaining the permission of their Scouter.

(k) A person who is not a Member of the Association is required to hold the appropriate Charge Certificate when in charge of craft in the course of a Scouting activity on Class B1, B2, B3 or A waters, unless the activity is approved by the holder of the appropriate Authorising Charge Certificate. This rule applies in the same way to such persons who are in charge of a group of three canoes.

(l) The requirement for holding a Charge Certificate does not apply:
- ☐ if the activity is authorised by a person holding the appropriate Authorising Charge Certificate, endorsed as necessary;
- ☐ when sailing or power craft are hired on an hourly basis.

(m) The requirement for holding an Authorising Charge Certificate does not apply when a leader is supervising Group activities in B1 or B2 waters. In such cases the leader will be required to have attended a 'Leadership and Supervisory Skills' course, approved by Headquarters, when his Charge Certificate will be endorsed 'Authority to Supervise'.

Rule 75 iii   Classification of Waters

(a) For the purpose of all water activities undertaken as Scouting activities, waters are classified as C, B1, B2, B3 and A, by County Water Activity Committees. A *National Directory of Waters* is published annually by Headquarters.

(b) A guide to the type of water expected to be found in these classifications is as follows:

Class C
Public boating ponds, etc.; some canals and other 'safe' inland waters.

Class B1
Sheltered inland waters and other sheltered waters where currents and tides create no real danger.

Class B2
The sea up to one mile from the shore, but excluding more dangerous waters close inshore; more sheltered parts of estuaries; large inland lakes and lochs; inland waters British Canoe Union Grade 2.

Class B3
The sea up to three miles from the shore, but excluding more dangerous waters close inshore; busy commercial ports; exposed parts of estuaries; inland waters British Canoe Union Grade 3.

Class A
Open sea more than three miles from the shore, and other dangerous waters close inshore; inland waters British Canoe Union Grade 4 and above.

(c) The classification of particular waters may vary at different times of the year.

(d) Where waters are not classified for any reason, or when carrying out water activities abroad, the leader responsible for the activity should assess and classify the waters in accordance with the guidance given in *Rule 75 iii (b) above*. No waters, other than shallow, still water and public boating ponds may be classified as C and no tidal waters may be classified as B1 or C.

(e) The issuing of Boat Certificates and Charge Certificates (with the necessary endorsements) entitles the holder to operate on waters of the class for which they were issued and on waters of lower classifications.

Rule 75 iv Lifejackets and Buoyancy Aids

(a) Lifejackets and buoyancy aids as required in the chart following must be provided for all Members of the Association or the crew of a vessel. Lifejackets must be of a pattern approved by the Department of the Environment or the British Standards Institute. Buoyancy aids must be of a pattern approved by the Ship and Boat Builders' National Federation.

Note: If in doubt, about the definition of craft, the Scouter should consult the appropriate Commissioner or Adviser.

(b) Lifejackets are to be worn in all boats where there is low visibility, rough weather or broken water. This rule does not apply when canoe surfing or in white water, provided that an approved buoyancy aid is worn in place of a lifejacket.

(c) Lifejackets are to be worn at all times by crews of rescue boats which are relatively high-speed boats. This rule does not apply to safety boats which are displacement vessels, suitable for general escort duties.

(d) Where a buoyancy aid is specified, a lifejacket may be substituted, but not vice versa.

(e) The person in charge of all activities may, at any time, insist on stricter requirements than listed.

(f) The wearing of lifejackets and buoyancy aids may be relaxed at the discretion of an Authorising Charge Certificate holder provided he

Lifejacket and Buoyancy Aid Chart

Scout Classification	C	B1	B2(non-tidal)	B2(tidal) & B3	A
Rowing	Not mandatory	Not mandatory	Lifejackets to be carried	Lifejackets to be worn	Lifejackets to be worn
Pulling	Not mandatory	Not mandatory	Lifejackets to be carried	Lifejackets to be carried	Lifejackets to be worn
Sailing (day boat)	Buoyancy aids to be worn	Buoyancy aids to be worn	Lifejackets to be carried	Lifejackets to be worn	Lifejackets to be carried
Sailing (cruisers)	Lifejackets to be carried	Lifejackets to be carried	Lifejackets to be carried	Lifejackets to be worn	Lifejackets to be carried
Canoes	Buoyancy aids to be worn	Buoyancy aids to be worn	Lifejackets to be worn (except when Rules II, 75 iv (b) and (f) apply)	Lifejackets to be worn (except when Rules II, 75 iv (b) and (f) apply)	Lifejackets to be carried
Powerboats (cruising)	Buoyancy aids to be carried, sufficient for a working crew	Buoyancy aids to be carried, sufficient for a working crew	Lifejackets to be worn	Lifejackets to be worn	Lifejackets to be carried
Powerboats (open planing)	Lifejackets to be worn	Lifejackets to be worn	Lifejackets to be worn	Lifejackets to be worn	Lifejackets to be worn
Powerboats (open displacement)	Not mandatory	Not mandatory	Lifejackets to be carried	Lifejackets to be carried	Lifejackets to be worn
Tender to another vessel	At the discretion of the skipper of the parent vessel				

is present, for activities in waters for which his qualifications are valid, e.g. while canoe surfing; when racing under British Canoe Union/Scottish Canoe Association rules; at canoe events where there are sufficient rescue facilities in the near vicinity.

(g) When intending to proceed into any exposed waters in canoes or open boats, *Rule II, 75 vii (b)* applies.

Rule 75 v Canoeing

(a) Canoes owned by or on long term loan to a Member or a unit of the Association must be covered by a valid Boat Certificate in accordance with *Rule 75 i above*.

(b) Before canoeing, Members of the Association must have sought advice on local conditions and know and understand any public warnings, regulations or bye-laws applying to the waters on which they are operating. Care should be taken to ensure that a legal right of way exists on the water in use and that the interests of other river users are respected.

(c) Lifejackets or buoyancy aids must be worn as specified in *Rule 75 iv above*.

(d) Members of the Association may not take part in canoeing unless they can comply with the swimming requirements shown in *Rule II, 75 xiv (g) and (h)*.

(e) For details of the classification of waters see *Rule 75 iii above*, and the *National Directory of Waters*, available from Headquarters.

(f) On all classes of water, canoeing must take place in groups of no less than three canoes unless there is sufficient safety cover.

(g) On Class B1, B2, B3 and A waters, at least one in every three members of the party must hold a Charge Certificate appropriate to the waters in question. On B1 waters a holder of a B2 Charge Certificate, who holds the Proficiency Award of the British Canoe Union may take charge of a party of up to six members.

(h) *Rule 75 v (g) above* does not apply if the activity is authorised by a person holding an Authorising Charge Certificate appropriate to the waters in question.

(i) A Charge Certificate need not be held by any member of the party when canoeing on Class C waters.

The following table shows the standard of qualification necessary to hold Charge Certificates and Authorising Charge Certificates for **Canoeing.**

Class of Water	Charge Certificate	Authorising Charge Certificate
C	None required	None required
B1 Inland	BCU 1 Star Test (Elementary)	BCU Inland Trainee Instructor
Sea	BCU 1 Star Test (Elementary)	BCU Sea Trainee Instructor
B2 Inland	BCU Inland Proficiency or BCU 3 Star Test	BCU Inland Instructor
Sea	BCU Inland Proficiency and tidal knowledge and experience (*See Note below*) or BCU 3 Star Test and tidal knowledge and experience (*See Note below*) or BCU Sea Proficiency	BCU Sea Instructor
B3 Inland	BCU Inland Proficiency	BCU Inland Senior Instructor
Sea	BCU Sea Proficiency	BCU Sea Senior Instructor
A Inland	BCU Advanced Inland Proficiency	BCU Inland Senior Instructor and BCU Advanced Inland Proficiency
Sea	BCU Advanced Sea Proficiency	BCU Sea Senior Instructor and BCU Advanced Sea Proficiency

(BCU refers to British Canoe Union)

Note: '*Tidal knowledge and experience*' *mentioned above in the B2 Charge Certificate should include an appreciation of the effects of tide and its dangers, tidal streams, observation and prediction of tides, tidal ranges, springs and neaps, overfalls, races, the effect of wind on tidal waters, and channels for vessels with deeper draughts.*

(j) Charge Certificates and Authorising Charge Certificates are obtained as described in *Rule 75 ii above.*

(k) Crash helmets and spray covers are to be worn by canoeists in white water, or in coastal surf. Crash helmets must be worn when playing bat polo.

(l) *Rule II, 75 vii* applies when canoeing more than 15 miles offshore.

(m) *Rule 73 v above* applies when canoeing abroad.

Rule 75 vi   Charter Vessels

(a) When vessels are hired or chartered, the activity rules of the Association apply with the exception of the requirement of a Boat Certificate, when *Rule 75 i (d) above* applies.

(b) Before entering into a hire agreement which includes an indemnity clause (i.e. where it is assumed that the hirer will be responsible for damage, injury or loss), the agreement must be referred to Headquarters.

(c) Where a vessel is chartered to be under the command of professional staff, the rules relating to Charge Certificates do not apply.

(d) When taking Members of the Association as passengers on hired sailing or powered craft, the leader responsible must:

☐ have reasonable grounds to believe that the person in charge of the craft, who must be either the owner or authorised by the owner, has the necessary knowledge, skill and experience;

☐ ensure that the party understands the discipline necessary for safety, including any local regulations or bye-laws which may apply.

Rule 75 vii   Offshore Boating

The following rules only apply if proceeding more than fifteen miles offshore.

(a) Members of the Association taking craft more than fifteen miles from shore must notify Headquarters of the intended cruise on form SB. Normal Coastguard procedures for reporting departures and arrivals in such cruises must be followed.

(b) On cruises as in *Rule 75 vii (a) above*, the following conditions must also be met:

☐ when canoeing, the group must include a minimum of two members holding Charge Certificates appropriate for the water in question, *Rule 75 v (h) above* notwithstanding;

☐ when boating, other than canoeing, one member of the crew of each vessel must hold a Charge Certificate appropriate to the water in question and another member of the crew must hold at least a Class A Mates' Charge Certificate, *Rule 75 ii (c) above* still applies;

☐ all open boats must be fitted with rigid buoyancy tanks or with built-in solid buoyancy;

☐ in canoes and open boats, lifejackets specified in *Rule 75 iv (a) above* must be of a type with minimum buoyancy of 6 kilogrammes (13½ lbs) which can be further inflated to 16 kilogrammes (35 lbs), or a minimum built-in buoyancy of 16 kilogrammes (35 lbs);

☐ distress signals must be carried;

☐ the Scouter or other person in charge of a group of canoes must consider carefully the need to be accompanied by one or more rescue boats.

(c) Where it is intended that a cruising vessel will proceed over fifteen miles offshore, it must be surveyed by a qualified surveyor once every three years.

Rule 75 viii   Powerboating

(a) Boats owned by or on long term loan to a Member or unit of the Association must be covered by a valid Boat Certificate in accordance with *Rule 75 i above.*

(b) All persons in charge of boats must have sought advice on local conditions and know and understand any public warnings, regulations or bye-laws applying to the waters on which they are operating.

(c) Lifejackets or buoyancy aids must be worn or carried as specified in *Rule 75 iv above.*

(d) Members of the Association may not take part in powerboating unless they can comply with the swimming requirements shown in *Rule II, 75 xiv (g) and (h).*

(e) For details of the classification of waters see *Rule 75 iii above,* and the *National Directory of Waters,* available from Headquarters.

(f) On Class B1, B2, B3 and A waters, the person in command of each vessel must hold a Charge Certificate appropriate to the waters in question.

(g) *Rule 75 viii (f) above* does not apply if the activity is authorised by a person holding an Authorising Charge Certificate, appropriate to the waters in question.

(h) A Charge Certificate need not be held when powerboating on Class C waters.

(i) The term 'Powerboats – restricted' as used in these rules refers typically to:
□ powerboats under 1000 cc, not capable of more than ten knots;
□ hired power cruisers on inland waters;
□ displacement powerboats not more than 6 metres length overall.

All powerboats that exceed the above specifications are referred to as 'Powerboats – unrestricted'.

(j) Charge Certificates and Authorising Charge Certificates are obtained as described in *Rule 75 ii above.*

The following table shows the standard of qualification necessary to hold Charge Certificates and Authorising Charge Certificates relating to **Powerboating – restricted.**

Class of Water	Charge Certificate	Authorising Charge Certificate
C	None required	None required
B1	Scout Association B1 Power Certificate	RYA National Motor Cruising Basic Certificate or RYA National Motor Launch and Powerboat Certificate – Grade 1 or RYA Coastal Certificate Grade 1
B2	Scout Association B2 Power Certificate	RYA National Motor Cruising Certificate with endorsement A or B *(See Note (i) below)* or RYA Motor Launch and Powerboat Certificate Grade 2
B3	RYA National Motor Cruising Certificate with endorsement A or B *(See Note (i) below)* or RYA Motor Launch and Powerboat Certificate Grade 2 or RYA Coastal Certificate Grade 2 or RYA Instructor Award or RYA Day Skipper/Watch Leader Certificate	RYA Yachtmaster (Offshore) Certificate – endorsed for powercraft only or RYA Offshore Log Book Grade 3

continued opposite

A	RYA/DoT Yachtmaster (Offshore) Certificate endorsed for power craft only or RYA/DoT Coastal Skipper Certificate *(See Note (ii) below)* or RYA Offshore Log Book Grade 3	RYA/DoT Yachtmaster Certificate – endorsed for power craft only or RYA Offshore Log Book Grade 3 *(See Note (i) below)*

(RYA refers to Royal Yachting Association, DoT refers to Department of Trade)

Notes:
(i) Where endorsements are required with the Motor Cruising Certificates, the endorsement A applies to inland waters, and the endorsement B to tidal waters.
(ii) Charge Certificates issued on the strength of this Certificate must be endorsed 'Valid for coastal, inshore and inland passage only'.

The following table shows the standard of qualification necessary to hold Charge Certificates and Authorising Charge Certificates relating to **Powerboating – unrestricted.**

Class of Water	Charge Certificate	Authorising Charge Certificate
C	None required	None required
B1	Power Coxswain Badge (equivalent standard for Leaders)	RYA National Motor Cruising Basic Certificate or RYA National Motor Launch and Powerboat Certificate Grade 1 or RYA Coastal Certificate Grade 1

continued on page 236

B2	RYA National Motor Cruising Basic Certificate or RYA Motor Launch and Powerboat Certificate Grade 1	RYA/DoT Yachtmaster (Offshore) Certificate endorsed for power craft only or RYA Offshore Log Book Grade 3 or RYA Sportsboat Certificate or RYA Instructor Award
B3	RYA National Motor Cruising Certificate with endorsement A or B *(See Note (i) below)* or RYA Sportsboat Certificate or RYA Motor Launch and Powerboat Certificate Grade 2 or RYA Coastal Certificate Grade 2 or RYA Instructor Award or RYA Day Skipper/Watch Leader Certificate	RYA Yachtmaster (Offshore) Certificate endorsed for power craft only or RYA Offshore Log Book Grade 3
A	RYA/DoT Yachtmaster (Offshore) Certificate endorsed for power craft only or RYA/DoT Coastal Skipper Certificate *(See Note (ii) below)* or RYA Offshore Log Book Grade 3	RYA/DoT Yachtmaster Certificate endorsed for power craft only or RYA Offshore Log Book Grade 3 *(See Note (i) below)*

(RYA refers to Royal Yachting Association, DoT refers to Department of Trade)

Notes:

(i) Where endorsements are required with the Motor Cruising Certi-

ficates, the endorsement A applies to inland waters, and the endorsement B to tidal waters.

(ii) Charge Certificates issued on the strength of this Certificate must be endorsed 'Valid for coastal, inshore and inland passage only'.

(k) The standard required for the issue of a Class A Mates' Charge Certificate for all powerboats is either RYA Offshore Certificate Grade 2 or RYA Coastal Certificate Grade 2 or RYA National Motor Cruising Certificate with endorsement B or RYA Sportsboat Certificate or RYA Motor Launch and Power Boat Certificate Grade 2 or RYA Day Skipper/Watch Leader Certificate.

(RYA refers to Royal Yachting Association.)

(l) *Rule 75 vii above* applies when powerboating more than fifteen miles offshore.

(m) *Rule 73 v above* applies when powerboating abroad.

Rule 75 ix   Pulling

(a) Boats owned by or on long term loan to a Member or unit of the Association must be covered by a valid Boat Certificate in accordance with *Rule 75 i above.*

(b) All persons in charge of boats must have sought advice on local conditions and know and understand any public warnings, regulations or bye-laws applying to the waters on which they are operating.

(c) Lifejackets or buoyancy aids must be worn or carried as specified in *Rule 75 iv above.*

(d) Members of the Association may not take part in pulling unless they can comply with the swimming requirements shown in *Rule II, 75 xiv (g) and (h).*

(e) For details of classification of waters see *Rule 75 iii above* and the *National Directory of Waters*, available from Headquarters.

(f) On Class B1, B2, B3 and A waters, the person in command of each vessel must hold a

Charge Certificate appropriate to the waters in question.

(g) *Rule 75 ix (f) above* does not apply if the activity is authorised by a person holding an Authorising Charge Certificate, appropriate to the waters in question.

(h) A Charge Certificate need not be held when pulling on Class C waters.

(i) Charge Certificates and Authorising Charge Certificates are obtained as described in *Rule 75 ii above*.

The following table shows the standard of qualification necessary to hold Charge Certificates and Authorising Charge Certificates relating to **Pulling**.

Class of Water	Charge Certificate	Authorising Charge Certificate
C	None required	None required
B1	Scout Association B1 Pulling Certificate *(See Note below)*	Scout Association B2 Pulling Certificate *(See Note below)*
B2	Scout Association B2 Pulling Certificate *(See Note below)*	Scout Association B3 Pulling Certificate *(See Note below)*
B3	Scout Association B3 Pulling Certificate *(See Note below)*	*(See Note below)*
A	*(See Note below)*	*(See Note below)*

Note: Any of the equivalent standards for Sailing or Powerboating for the same class of waters are acceptable as alternatives.

(j) The standard required for the issue of a Class A Mates' Charge Certificate for pulling boats is either RYA Offshore Log Book Grade 2, or RYA Coastal Certificate Grade 2, or RYA Advanced Day Boat Certificate, or RYA National Motor Cruising Certificate with endorsement B, or RYA Sportsboat Certificate or RYA Motor Launch and Power Boat Certificate Grade 2.

(RYA refers to Royal Yachting Association)

(k) *Rule 75 vii above* applies when pulling more than fifteen miles offshore.

(l) *Rule 73 v above* applies when pulling abroad.

Rule 75 x   Rafting

(a) Rafts, except when used as described in *Rule II, 75 x (b)*, are not subject to the requirements of Boat Certificates or the Charge Certificate scheme. They should be used at the discretion of the Scouter concerned.

(b) Rafts used for overnight expeditions or for expeditions of more than ten miles, will require inspection and certification before use in accordance with *Rule 75 i (a) above*. One member of the crew will require a Pulling Charge Certificate appropriate to the waters in question.

(c) Members of the Association may not take part in rafting unless they can comply with the swimming requirements shown in *Rule II, 75 xiv (g) and (h)*.

Rule 75 xi   Rescue and Safety Boats (Power)

(a) Vessels being used as either rescue or safety boats are subject to the rules appropriate to the type of boat.

(b) Rescue boats, so designated because they are high speed vessels capable of effecting an emergency rescue with the minimum of delay, should carry emergency rescue equipment, and all the crew should be qualified for the activity on the class of water concerned, except when undergoing training in rescue. The crew should at all times, even when standing by, be fully equipped and wearing lifejackets.

(c) Safety boats are those that accompany a training session or expedition in other types of craft, and act as a parent vessel to the activity.

In this case, the safety boat is expected to carry additional equipment and rations, in addition to acting as a safety boat.

Rule 75 xii   Rowing

(a) When handling boats under oars, *Rule 75 ix above* applies. This includes sculling over the stern.

(b) When rowing in eights, fours and sculls, the normal standards and control of the Amateur Rowing Association apply instead of the rules of The Scout Association.

Note: This only applies to the specialist craft, similar to those used competitively at events organised by the Amateur Rowing Association.

Rule 75 xiii   Sailing (Day Boat and Cruising)

(a) Boats owned by or on long term loan to a Member or unit of the Association must be covered by a valid Boat Certificate in accordance with *Rule 75 i above.*

(b) All persons in charge of boats must have sought advice on local conditions and know and understand any public warnings, regulations or bye-laws applying to the waters on which they are operating.

(c) Lifejackets or buoyancy aids must be worn or carried as specified in *Rule 75 iv above.*

(d) Members of the Association may not take part in sailing unless they can comply with the swimming requirements shown in *Rule II, 75 xiv (g) and (h).*

(e) For details of the classification of waters see *Rule 75 iii above* and the *National Directory of Waters*, available from Headquarters.

(f) On Class B1, B2, B3 and A waters, the person in command of each vessel must hold a Charge Certificate appropriate to the waters in question.

(g) *Rule 75 xiii (f) above* does not apply if the

activity is authorised by a person holding an Authorising Charge Certificate, appropriate to the waters in question.

(h) A Charge Certificate need not be held when sailing on Class C waters.

(i) The term 'Day Boat' in these rules is intended to refer to vessels for which the Royal Yachting Association's National Day Boat scheme is appropriate. This would not normally include vessels over 20 ft. or with built in accommodation. These vessels would be classed as 'Cruising Vessels'. County Water Activity Committees should be consulted if there is any doubt.

Note: Some very small cruising vessels may be classed as 'Day Boats' or 'Cruising Vessels' for the purpose of these rules, at the discretion of the County Water Activities Committee.

(j) Charge Certificates and Authorising Charge Certificates are obtained as described in *Rule 75 ii above.*

The following table shows the standard of qualification necessary to hold Charge Certificates and Authorising Charge Certificates relating to sailing **Day Boats with or without auxiliary motors**.

Class of Water	Charge Certificate	Authorising Charge Certificate
C	None required	None required
B1	RYA Elementary Day Boat Certificate	RYA Advanced Day Boat Certificate
B2	RYA Intermediate Day Boat Certificate	RYA Instructor Award
B3	RYA Advanced Day Boat Certificate	RYA Senior Instructor Award or NSSA Sailing Master Award

continued on page 242

Class of Water	Charge Certificate	Authorising Charge Certificate
A	This activity may only be undertaken on the authority of a person holding the appropriate Authorising Charge Certificate	RYA/DoT Yachtmaster (Offshore) Certificate and RYA Advanced Day Boat Certificate or RYA Offshore Log Book Grade 3 and RYA Advanced Day Boat Certificate

(RYA refers to Royal Yachting Association, DoT refers to Department of Trade, NSSA refers to National School Sailing Association.)

Note: Where a 'Day Boat' Sailing Certificate is for use in tidal waters, the appropriate tidal endorsement must have been gained for the RYA Certificate as well as the Charge Certificate.

The following table shows the standard of qualification necessary to hold Charge Certificates and Authorising Charge Certificates relating to sailing **Cruising Vessels with or without auxiliary motors**.

Class of Water	Charge Certificate	Authorising Charge Certificate
C	None required	None required
B1	RYA Coastal Certificate Grade 1 or RYA Day Skipper/Watch Leader Certificate	RYA/DoT Yachtmaster (Offshore) Certificate or RYA Offshore Log Book Grade 3
B2	RYA Coastal Certificate Grade 1 or RYA Offshore Log Book Grade 2 or RYA Day Skipper/Watch Leader Certificate	RYA/DoT Yachtmaster (Offshore) Certificate or RYA Offshore Log Book Grade 3
B3	RYA Coastal Certificate Grade 2 or RYA Day Skipper/Watch Leader Certificate	RYA/DoT Yachtmaster (Offshore) Certificate or RYA Offshore Log Book Grade 3

continued opposite

| A | RYA/DoT Yachtmaster (Offshore) Certificate or RYA Offshore Log Book Grade 3 or RYA/DoT Coastal Skipper Certificate *(See Note (ii) below)* | RYA/DoT Yachtmaster (Offshore) Instructor |

Notes:
(i) An alternative qualification is available for cruising vessels under sail on inland waters. This is issued under the authority of County Water Activities Committees, and the syllabus is obtainable from Head-quarters.
(ii) Charge Certificates issued on the strength of this Certificate must be endorsed 'Valid for coastal, inshore and inland passage only'.

(k) The standard required for the issue of a Class A Mates' Charge Certificate for Cruising Vessels under sail, with or without an auxiliary motor, is the RYA Offshore Log Book Grade 2 or RYA Coastal Certificate Grade 2 or RYA Advanced Day Boat Certificate or RYA Day Skipper/Watch Leader Certificate.
(RYA refers to Royal Yachting Association.)
(l) *Rule 75 vii above* applies, when intending sailing more than fifteen miles offshore.
(m) *Rule 73 v above* applies, when sailing abroad.

Rule 75 xiv   Swimming
(a) Before permitting swimming by Cub Scouts or Scouts, the Scouter or other person responsible must consider all the circumstances including:
□ the age, experience, ability and state of health of each Cub Scout or Scout;
□ the suitability of the water in respect of its

depth, cleanliness and the movement of any tide, current or undertow;
□ the weather conditions;
□ the number of participants.

(b) The person responsible must post a picket of two good swimmers in such a place as to be able to give immediate help in cases of emergency. The pickets must be equipped with a lifeline and must be suitably dressed ready to take appropriate action immediately.

(c) An emergency signal (e.g. short blasts on a whistle) must be arranged and the swimmers must be briefed to leave the water on hearing this signal.

(d) Parties of swimmers must be so organised that they swim in groups of two or three. These groups should stay together and if one of the swimmers gets into difficulty, the other(s) can raise the alarm.

(e) The posting of pickets and the use of the Buddy System as required by *Rule 75 xiv (d) above* does not apply if there is clearly no need for such precautions (e.g. in public swimming baths).

(f) When swimming with Cub Scouts or Scouts, Venture Scouts should apply all the precautions set out in these rules.

(g) Members of the Association taking part in any other water activity, must be able to demonstrate to a suitable person (e.g. a Scouter) their ability to swim 50 metres in ordinary clothes, and keep afloat for 5 minutes. This may be relaxed at the discretion of the Scouter in charge when using recognised forms of public transport; or when it is clearly unnecessary (e.g. on very shallow boating ponds).

(h) In the case where Members of the Association are unable to attain the requirements laid down in *Rule 75 xiv (g) above*, the Scouter may at his discretion relax this rule, providing that the Scout concerned is wearing a life-jacket (except when below decks or protected in larger vessels) *and* in the charge of an adult *and* the only non-swimmer in the boat.

Note: If in any doubt, the Scouter should consult the appropriate Commissioner or Adviser.

Rule 75 xv   Sub-Aqua

Underwater activities should be carried out using the standards and controls laid down by the British Sub-Aqua Club or Scottish Sub-Aqua Club; or under the control of a Member of the Association having the appropriate Charge Certificate for the type of boat being used, and conducting the activity in accordance with the standards of the British Sub-Aqua Club or Scottish Sub-Aqua Club.

Rule 75 xvi   Tenders to Other Vessels

Tenders to other vessels usually are small pulling boats or small boats with small outboard motors, and in the main they are used to ferry personnel and equipment from shore to ship. There is still a requirement for a Boat Certificate, see *Rule 75 i above*, but the boat may be crewed by personnel at the discretion of the skipper of the parent vessel.

Rule 75 xvii   Water Skiing

Water skiing should be carried out using the standards and controls laid down by the British Water Ski Federation; or under the control of a Member of the Association having the appropriate Charge Certificate for powerboating, see *Rule 75 viii above*, and conducting the activity in accordance with the standards of the British Water Ski Federation.

Rule 76 — Other Activities and Pursuits

Rule 76 i   Aerial Runways

(a) Aerial runways must only be constructed under the personal supervision of an experienced and responsible leader, who must also supervise the operation of the runway.

(b) The leader in charge of the activity must ensure that:

☐ a hawser, tested for soundness, of 24 mm diameter, made of manila, sisal, staple spun polypropylene, polyester or nylon, is used;

☐ the seat is purpose-built and securely attached to the eye of a single sheave block. In no circumstances may a block with a hook be used;

☐ all equipment is checked before use;

☐ the height and the angle of the slope is such that a safe, steady descent is possible;

☐ the entire structure is checked regularly during the activity for safety.

(c) Aerial runways must not be used by members of the general public under any circumstances.

Note: More details concerning the construction of aerial runways is contained in The Aerial Runway Code, *obtainable from Headquarters.*

Rule 76 ii   Archery

Archery should be carried out using the standards and controls laid down by the Grand National Archery Society, as laid down in *Rules of Shooting* available from Headquarters.

Rule 76 iii   Martial Arts

Aikido, Chinese and Korean Martial Arts, Jiu-Jitsu, Karate and Kendo should be carried out using the standards and controls laid down by the Martial Arts Commission.

Rule 76 iv   Riding

Activities involving horse riding or pony trekking should be carried out using the standards and controls of the British Horse Society, and laid down in *The Riding Code*, available from Headquarters.

Rule 76 v   Shooting

(a) No firearms, airguns or shotguns may be acquired, held or used by any Scout unit unless the Group Scout Leader has ascertained, understands and complies with any statutory requirements or bye-laws relating to their possession, use and registration. A licence issued by the Police is needed for the possession of firearms and shotguns.

(b) Members of the Association may practise shooting with firearms or airguns of greater than .177 (4.5 mm) calibre, or take part in shooting matches only at ranges provided by a local authority or by one of the armed services or, as members, at a club approved for the purpose laid down by Act of Parliament. The activity must be supervised by a Range Officer who will be responsible to see that all participants comply with the range rules.

(c) Members of the Association may practise shooting with airguns of .177 (4.5 mm) calibre or take part in shooting matches only at ranges properly constructed to comply with local bye-laws and the rules of the National Small-bore Rifle Association. The activity must be supervised by a competent leader or authorised helper, who has knowledge of correct use of airguns, and who will be responsible to see that the following range rules are obeyed:

☐ the range, except during specified hours for firing, is out of bounds;

☐ no one will be allowed to load the rifle until in position on the firing point and have received an order to do so;

- [ ] no one shall point the rifle in any direction other than at the butts;
- [ ] the range must be so constructed that access to the firing area (that part of the range between firing point and butts) is not possible whilst shooting is in progress;
- [ ] all windows in the range area must be protected with material capable of stopping a .177 pellet at short range;
- [ ] bullet catchers/target holders must be metal-lined and backed and capable of stopping and retaining a .177 pellet. Suitable holders are available from the National Small-bore Rifle Association.

(d) Firearms or airguns may only be taken on to Scout premises, camp sites, camps or on Scout projects or expeditions if prior permission in writing has been obtained, both from the home District Commissioner and from the person authorised to be in charge of the premises, camp site, camp, project or expedition, and if adequate arrangements for the safeguarding of the firearms or airguns in a locked cupboard or similar safe place has been made. Permission may be given only if the firearms or airguns are being transported or are in transit under supervision for use as permitted in *Rule 76 v (a), (b) and (c) above.*

(e) In no circumstances may any person handling a firearm or airgun at any Scout premises, camp site, camp or on a Scout project or expedition, indulge in indiscriminate firing.

Safety Rules for Joint Adventurous Activities

Mixed activities are a part of the programme for both The Scout and The Girl Guides Associations, especially for the Venture Scout and Ranger Guide Sections, and the following Rules are designed to ensure responsible leadership by adults in these activities.

Leaders should recognise the responsibility they have towards their members, giving them the encouragement and protection demanded by their age and experience, particularly on those occasions when Scouts and Guides are involved (who must be over the age of 11), but at the same time recognising the fact that young people need opportunities to exercise responsibility in the management of their own affairs. This is especially true in the Venture Scout and Ranger Guide Sections, but as a principle it should also be kept in mind when working with Scouts and Guides.

The following Rules have been designed on the basis of the existing conditions which each Association sets for its members in relation to adventurous activities. They are the basic rules recognised by the two Associations for joint participation in these activities.

In these rules, the words "Scouter/Guider" shall be taken to infer that responsibility for any adventurous activities shall be held jointly. However, where leaders themselves do not have the requisite specialist skills for a particular activity, this responsibility must be delegated to a suitably qualified person provided that that person has been approved by the District Commissioners.

The words "Scout/Guides" mean members of either Association over the age of 11 who are not adult leaders or Instructors. The insurance arrangements and cover varies for each Association for these activities and leaders must, therefore, be aware of their own Association's insurance requirements.

For adventurous activities not included in these Rules, leaders should, in consultation with their respective District Commissioners, refer to the Safety Rules of National Organisations for advice and guidance before participating in those activities.

Responsibilities of Commissioners

Responsibility for authorising adventurous activities on a joint basis rests with the respective District Commissioners whose authority must be obtained by the Scouters or Guiders involved before any Scouts and Guides undertake such activities within their programme.

In giving such authority, the District Commissioners must be satisfied that the Scouters and Guiders involved (whether Leaders, Assistant Leaders, or Instructors) understand the relevant Safety Rules and that those specifically concerned with the leadership in the adventurous activity have the necessary training and experience, and are fully aware of their responsibilities. The authorisation will be given to the Scouters and Guiders in charge who will remain generally responsible to their respective District Commissioners. For each specialist activity the actual responsibility of leadership will be exercised by the most suitably qualified person who must be approved by both District Commissioners as the responsible leader for that adventurous activity. In certain circumstances, the District Commissioners may give authority to adequately qualified and competent leaders jointly to carry out specific activities for a defined period and/or area before seeking renewed authority.

Leaders once authorised should work on the basis of mutual consultation and wherever possible offer joint leadership in these activities. These consultations with 'opposite numbers' form an important aspect of the leadership role.

Air Activities

Before permitting certain air activities Scouters/Guiders must ensure that the following conditions are complied with:

1 Insurance

(i) All aircraft must be insured to legal requirements;

(ii) Members of The Girl Guides Association who take control or part control of an aircraft or glider must make the necessary insurance arrangements as they are not covered in any way by their Association's insurance.

2 Permission

A Scout/Guide under the age of 18 must have written permission to fly, signed by the parent or guardian.

3 Access

Before proceeding on to any airfield, the person responsible must

(i) Have permission from the controlling authority;

(ii) Have obtained an adequate briefing of the airfield layout, movement of planes and all possible dangers;

(iii) Have subsequently briefed the party for

which he/she is responsible.

Note: The foregoing Rules do not apply to visits to civil airports when the spectators' enclosure is used, or to Service establishments on an Open Day.

4 Flying (Power or Gliding)

The pilot or instructor must be qualified either by the Department of Trade (Flying) or the British Gliding Association (Gliding) to fly passengers or pupils in the type of aircraft used.

Bathing

1 Before giving permission to Scouts/Guides to bathe it is the responsibility of the Scouter/Guider to:

(i) Consider all the circumstances including:

(a) The age, experience and ability of each member of the party and whether his/her health allows him/her to bathe;

(b) The depth, temperature and state of the water at the time;

(c) The weather conditions;

(d) The number of bathers – in relation to the above these may need to be restricted;

(ii) Post a picket of two good swimmers for every 25 bathers. One of the pickets must hold the Bronze Medallion (or higher qualification) of either the Royal Life Saving Society or the Surf Life Saving Association, renewed within five years. The pickets must be equipped with a lifeline, wear bathing dress under a coat, and be in a position (e.g. in a boat or on a bank) to give immediate help in the case of emergency;

(iii) Arrange an emergency signal (e.g. short blasts on a whistle) on hearing which all bathers will leave the water;

(iv) Ensure that in the case of parties bathing a 'pairing' system is used;

(v) Take every precaution that would be taken by a reasonable and prudent parent; in any case where there can be any doubt as to the precautions necessary, the local District Commissioners or other persons experienced in swimming and familiar with the bathing place must be consulted.

Note: The rules in paragraphs (ii), (iii) and (iv) above may be relaxed only in properly supervised swimming baths and on beaches where another organisation (e.g. the Royal Life Saving Society) is in overall charge.

Boating and Canoeing

1 (i) Scouts/Guides taking part in any boating activity must be able to demonstrate to a suitable person, e.g. Scouter/Guider, his/her ability to swim 50 metres in ordinary clothes, and keep afloat for 5 minutes. This clause may be relaxed at the discretion of the Scouter/Guider in charge when:

(a) Using recognised forms of public transport;

(b) It is clearly unnecessary, e.g. on very shallow boating pools.

(ii) In the case of Scouts/Guides unable to attain the requirements laid down in 1(i) the Scouter/Guider may at his/her discretion relax this rule providing that the Scout/Guide concerned:

(a) Is wearing a lifejacket (except when below decks or protected in larger vessels);

(b) Is in the charge of an adult; and

(c) Is the only non-swimmer in the boat.

Note: If in any doubt the Scouter/Guider should consult the appropriate Commissioner or Adviser.

(iii) When taking Scouts/Guides as passengers on hired sailing or powered craft, the Scouter/Guider responsible must:

(a) Have reasonable grounds to believe that the person in charge of the craft, who is either the owner or authorised by the owner, has the necessary knowledge, skill and experience;

(b) Ensure that the party understands the discipline necessary for safety, including any local regulations or bye-laws which may apply.

2 Knee or thigh boots other than those designed specifically for boating must not be worn in boats.

3   (i) (a) Lifejackets approved by the Department of the Environment or the British Standards Institute,

   or (b) Buoyancy aids approved by the Ship and Boat Builders' National Federation, must be provided in accordance with the *Lifejacket and Buoyancy Aid Chart* opposite.

Note: If in any doubt about the definition of craft, the Scouter/Guider should consult the appropriate Commissioner or Adviser.

   (ii) (a) Lifejackets are to be worn in all boats in low visibility, rough weather or broken water;

Note: This rule may be relaxed at the discretion of the Scouter/Guider when canoe surfing, provided that an approved buoyancy aid is worn in place of a lifejacket.

   (b) Lifejackets are to be worn at all times by crews of rescue boats, which are relatively high-speed boats ready to go to assist when required;

Note: This rule does not apply to safety boats which are displacement vessels suitable for general escort duties.

Lifejacket and Buoyancy Aid Chart

Girl Guide Classification:	Non-classified	B1	B2(A)	B2(B)	B3	A	Non-swimmers
Scout Classification:	C	B1	B2 (non-tidal)	B2 (tidal)	B3	A	Non-swimmers
Rowing	Not required	Not required	Lifejackets to be worn	Lifejackets to be worn	Lifejackets to be worn	Lifejackets to be worn	Rule 2 of the Boating and Canoeing Rules applies
Pulling	Not required	Not required	Lifejackets to be carried	Lifejackets to be worn	Lifejackets to be carried	Lifejackets to be worn	
Sailing (day boat)	Buoyancy aids to be worn	Lifejackets to be carried	Lifejackets to be carried	Lifejackets to be worn	Lifejackets to be worn	Lifejackets to be worn	
Sailing (cruisers)	Lifejackets to be carried	Lifejackets to be carried	Lifejackets to be carried	Lifejackets to be worn	Lifejackets to be worn	Lifejackets to be worn	
Canoes	Buoyancy aids to be worn	Lifejackets to be carried	Lifejackets to be carried	Lifejackets to be worn	Lifejackets to be worn	Lifejackets to be worn	
Powerboats (cruising)	Buoyancy aids to be carried, sufficient for a working crew	Buoyancy aids to be carried, sufficient for a working crew	Buoyancy aids to be carried, sufficient for a working crew	Lifejackets to be carried	Lifejackets to be carried	Lifejackets to be carried	
Powerboats (open planing)	Lifejackets to be worn	Lifejackets to be worn	Lifejackets to be worn	Lifejackets to be worn	Lifejackets to be worn	Lifejackets to be worn	
Powerboats (open displacement)	Not required	Not required	Not required	Lifejackets to be carried	Lifejackets to be carried	Lifejackets to be worn	
Tender to another vessel	At the discretion of the skipper of the parent vessel						

(c) Where a buoyancy aid is specified, a lifejacket may be substituted;

(d) The person in charge of all activities may at anytime insist on stricter requirements than listed;

(e) The wearing of lifejackets and buoyancy aids may be relaxed at the discretion of a Scouter holding an Authorising Charge Certificate for Class B2, B3 and A waters, or a Guider holding a Canoe Charge Permit (Sections 2 or 3) for activities in waters for which his or her qualifications are valid (e.g. canoe surfing, when racing under British Canoe Union/Scottish Canoe Association rules; at canoe events where there are sufficient rescue facilities in the near vicinity);

(iii) Crash helmets and spray covers are to be worn by canoeists in white water or in coastal surf;

(iv) In fully-decked craft safety harnesses must be worn by all those on deck at night but lifejackets need be worn only when ordered by the person in charge of the craft.

4 A boat, when in use, whether or not the property of a Unit, must be in charge of:

(i) A member holding the qualification of either Association valid for the boat and water in question;

or

(ii) A qualified person outside either Association whom the Scouter/Guider responsible is satisfied has the necessary knowledge, skill and experience.

5 Any boat owned by or on long-term loan to a unit of the Associations:

(i) Must be examined annually for seaworthiness and suitability for the purpose for which it is to be used;

(ii) Must be covered by a valid Certificate of Seaworthiness issued by one of the Associations.

Note: For The Girl Guides Association examiners are appointed by the appropriate Commissioner, after consultation with the Adviser for Boating Activities in the County. Annual Boat Certificates are obtainable through the Adviser for Boating Activities in the County. For The Scout Association Certificates are issued by the County Water Activities Committee.

6 The Scouter/Guider responsible must make certain that the boat carries all necessary equipment, that it is not overloaded, and not so stowed as to hinder its free working.

7 Where the holder of a boating qualification has not recently put his/her boating into practice, the appropriate Commissioner or Adviser must ensure that his/her skill and knowledge is up to the currently approved standard.

8 A Scout/Guide holding a boating qualification may not boat without the knowledge of the Scouter/Guider responsible on the day concerned.

Note: This rule may be relaxed at the discretion of the Scouter/Guider for stretches of safe, inland waters.

9 Guides under the age of 18 must obtain the written consent of a parent or guardian before undertaking racing, or racing training, in either rowing or canoeing.

Hillwalking/ Mountaineering/ Ski-ing

1 The Commissioners

(i) Before authorising these activities the Commissioners concerned must ensure that:

(a) The Scouter/Guider in overall charge of the party understands the responsibilities of leadership and the application of these Rules;

(b) The suitably qualified adult (if different from the leader authorised in (i) above) directly responsible for leading the actual activity has had the required training experience, and understands the responsibilities he or she undertakes (see paragraphs 4, 5 and 6).

(ii) The authorising Commissioners or nominees whom he/she may have appointed will be responsible for notifying parents or guardians in the event of an accident or emergency and be able to receive reports from the Communicator (see paragraphs 5 (vi) and 7).

2 Application

The Safety Rules which follow apply in three distinct areas:

(i) To those parties in areas, usually below 610 metres (2,000 ft.) not covered in section (ii) below, that offer little protection against wind/rain/cold/snow under inclement weather conditions. Leaders must ensure that joint parties in these areas, which include the Fens, Downs, Wolds, Hills, Plains, Moors, Heaths, Forests and waste land, are equipped as for the more obviously 'potentially hazardous' country described in (ii) below when the weather conditions and/or the time of year make this necessary.

(ii) To those parties in the following areas where bad weather is normal, and good weather the exception:

England

Dartmoor, Exmoor, Bodmin Moor

The Peak District and The Pennines

The Cheviot Hills

The North Yorkshire Moors

The Lake District and the Cumbrian Mountains

Wales

The Cambrian Mountains

Snowdonia and North Wales generally

Mid Wales

South Wales

Brecon Beacons and Black Mountains

The Isle of Man

Scotland

The Southern Uplands

The Grampians and the North West Highlands

The Inner and Outer Hebrides

Orkney and Shetland

Ireland

The Sperrin Mountains and North Antrim Hills, Mourne Mountains and those other areas termed mountains in the Irish Republic; Other similar areas not defined above also qualify under this heading.

(iii) To those parties on hill/mountaineering expeditions abroad. In these cases the Safety Rules need to be augmented by considerably more experience and training, especially in snow/ice techniques, and the use of local and/or professional guides should be carefully considered.

Note: When an experienced Scouter/Guider is in charge of a party ski-ing in the vicinity of an estab-

lished ski piste or a working public chairlift or tow with which they are familiar, the following must be noted:

(i) The rules in paragraphs 5 *(vi)* and *(vii)* may be relaxed at his/her discretion;

(ii) The rules in paragraphs 5 *(viii)* and 6 *(ii)* will most probably not apply;

(iii) The whole of the rule in paragraph 7 must be followed in the event of a member of the party requiring assistance. In cases of accidents abroad immediate attention to paragraph 7 *(i)* is essential.

3 The Party

(i)(a) No expedition in potentially hazardous country should ever be undertaken alone or in pairs; a party should consist of not less than four, although in exceptional circumstances this may be reduced to three. Ten is the maximum party size, which must include two experienced adult leaders, and this is advisable only with low-level journeys;

(b) With larger numbers, separate parties must be formed each with adequate experienced and trained leadership;

(c) For higher and/or longer and/or snow/ice type expeditions six is the optimum number, including two adult leaders.

(ii) Activities as in paragraph 3 (i) (c) should not be undertaken without appropriate extra skills and equipment.

(iii) The suitably qualified adult must ensure that all the activities undertaken are well within the technical competence and physical capability of each member of the party.

4 Experience

The suitably qualified adult may not take or be responsible for Scouts/Guides in any of the three areas where the Safety Rules apply (see paragraph 3) unless he/she holds the appropriate Mountain Leadership Certificate or has had the following minimum experience:

(i) He/she should have acquired and studied the Mountain Rescue Committee's Handbook *Mountain Rescue and Cave Rescue* and The Sports Council's *Safety on Mountains*;

(ii) He/she should have climbed at least ten different hills over 610 metres (2,000 ft.) during the last two years. At least one week should have been spent under some form of instruction either from experienced friends, mountain guides, or on a Sports Council or other climbing school course; or on a series of climbing club "meets for beginners" equivalent to seven days.

Note: These requirements are the ideal, although suitable equivalents can be substituted where applicable. The areas intended for joint activities should be of a standard well within this experience.

(iii) He/she should have had previous experience and have understanding of the conditions likely to be encountered, especially cold, mist, rain, highwinds, ice and snow;

Note: Quickly worsening weather, particularly in Scotland, and innocent-looking ice and snow on beaten tracks at Christmas and Easter are among the most lethal of all the conditions likely to be experienced;

(iv) He/she must be competent in the use of map and compass in rain, mist and bad weather conditions in the mountains;

(v) He/she must be competent in route planning and navigation skills;

(vi) He/she must have a knowledge of the problem of hypothermia (exposure), must be able to take action to prevent it, and be able to recognise the signs and know the treatment.

5 Leadership

The suitably qualified adult in charge of the activity must:

(i) Read, study and apply the relevant recommendations relating to all aspects of the activity as in the most recent edition of *Safety on Mountains* (The Sports Council);

(ii) Comply with these Safety Rules;

(iii) Ensure that individual Scouts and Guides have received the necessary training and are conversant with *Safety on Mountains*;

(iv) Ensure that each party conforms to the conditions laid down in paragraphs 4, 5 and 6;

(v) Obtain from all members of the party the name, address and telephone number of their next of kin/guardian for use in case of emergency. In addition provide for the parents or guardians of each member aged between 11 and 18 essential details about the activity and obtain from them their written consent for the Scout/Guide concerned to participate;

(vi) Appoint a reliable person as "The Communicator", who should not be a close relative of any member of the party, and whose duties are to liaise, as appropriate, with the police, rescue organisations, the "host" and "home" Scout/Guide authorities and next of kin. In the case of small parties of not more than eight members this responsibility may be delegated to the Warden of a hostel, staff of a mountain rescue post, local police station or similar establishment but to ensure their effectiveness in the event of an accident or emergency they must have full details of route(s), timings, emergency equipment carried, and an accurate list of names and addresses of appropriate home contacts of all personnel in the party. In the case of a large party the "Communicator" should not be actively engaged on that part of the expedition for which he/she is acting as the "Communicator";

(vii) Give the "Communicator" the name, address and telephone number of the authorising Commissioners (or their nominees) as in paragraph 1 (ii);

(viii) Have had, or appoint someone who has had, recent experience of climbs of comparable standard when rock climbing is in the programme. On single-pitch outcrops the maximum number is six persons to one leader and second, and on multi-pitch climbs the maximum is three persons on a rope.

6 Accident Procedure

Neglect of the rules in paragraph 8 could lead to accidents. The leader of any party which experiences an accident or emergency must arrange for:

(i) Accident/mountain rescue procedures to be initiated;

(ii) The Communicator to be told about the accident/emergency and given the names of the member(s) of the party requiring assistance.

7 Having completed the procedure laid down in paragraph 9 the leader concerned or by then, more probably, the Communicator, will:

(i) Contact the authorising Commissioners or nominees, giving names and telephone numbers of the next of kin/guardians of those who required assistance;

(ii) Notify the host Scout/Guide authorities of the accident or emergency;

(iii) Maintain the link already established with the authorising Commissioners or nominees.

8 Over-riding Controls

(i) Normal 'permission to camp' arrangements must be carried out by members of each Association.

(ii) The County or District Commissioners in any area where such activities take place, or other authorised representatives, have an over-riding authority:

(a) To ensure that these Rules are followed;

(b) To direct that any particular activities shall be stopped or cancelled, if in their view it is essential in the interest of safety.

The Positions of Badges on Uniforms

Cub Scout

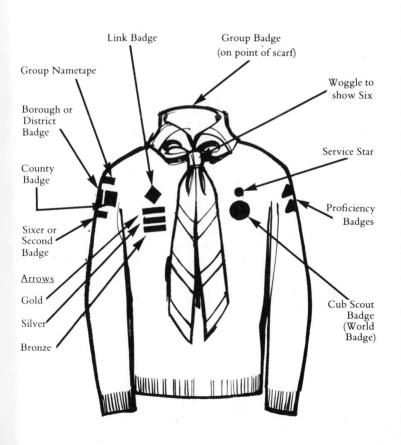

Link Badge

Group Badge
(on point of scarf)

Group Nametape

Woggle to
show Six

Borough or
District
Badge

Service Star

County
Badge

Proficiency
Badges

Sixer or
Second
Badge

<u>Arrows</u>

Gold

Silver

Cub Scout
Badge
(World
Badge)

Bronze

Scout

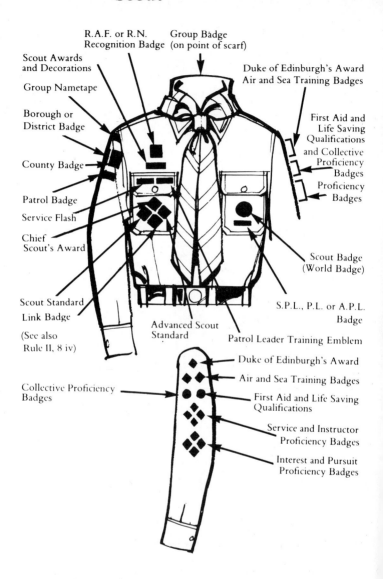

R.A.F. or R.N.
Recognition Badge

Group Badge
(on point of scarf)

Scout Awards
and Decorations

Group Nametape

Borough or
District Badge

County Badge

Patrol Badge

Service Flash

Chief
Scout's Award

Scout Standard
Link Badge

(See also
Rule II, 8 iv)

Duke of Edinburgh's Award
Air and Sea Training Badges

First Aid and
Life Saving
Qualifications
and Collective
Proficiency
Badges

Proficiency
Badges

Scout Badge
(World Badge)

S.P.L., P.L. or A.P.L.
Badge

Advanced Scout
Standard

Patrol Leader Training Emblem

Duke of Edinburgh's Award

Air and Sea Training Badges

First Aid and Life Saving
Qualifications

Collective Proficiency
Badges

Service and Instructor
Proficiency Badges

Interest and Pursuit
Proficiency Badges

Venture Scout

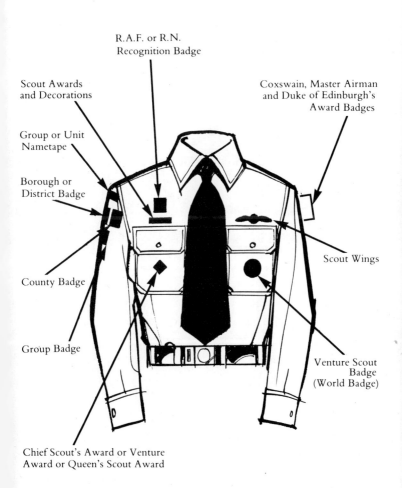

R.A.F. or R.N.
Recognition Badge

Scout Awards
and Decorations

Group or Unit
Nametape

Borough or
District Badge

County Badge

Group Badge

Coxswain, Master Airman
and Duke of Edinburgh's
Award Badges

Scout Wings

Venture Scout
Badge
(World Badge)

Chief Scout's Award or Venture
Award or Queen's Scout Award

Adult Leader

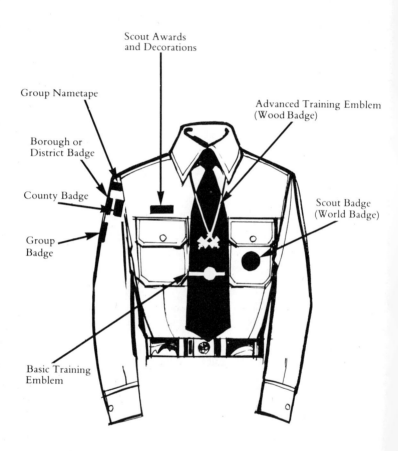

Scout Awards
and Decorations

Group Nametape

Borough or
District Badge

County Badge

Group
Badge

Advanced Training Emblem
(Wood Badge)

Scout Badge
(World Badge)

Basic Training
Emblem

Amendments

Amendments

Amendments

Amendments

Amendments

Amendments

Amendments

Amendments

Amendments

Amendments

Amendments

Amendments

Amendments

Amendments

Directory

301

N.B. *Passim* as used in this Directory denotes references throughout both Volumes which are too numerous to detail individually.